Tricia Guild in town

Contemporary design for urban living

Photography - Gilles de Chabaneix

Text - Elspeth Thompson

RIZZOLI
NEW YORK

For S.J. and S.J.

First published in the United States of America in 1996 by
Rizzoli International Publications Inc.
300 Park Avenue South, New York, NY 10010

First published in 1996 by
Quadrille Publishing Limited, London

ISBN 0-8478-1977-9
LC 96-68509

Printed and bound by Mohndruck Graphische
Betriebe GmbH, Germany

Special thanks to those who have generously allowed us to photograph their homes – Richard Polo for our house – Simon and Alison Jeffreys for their colorful town house – Lisa Guild for her serene apartment – Maureen Missner and John Venema for their artistic brownstone – Jo Willer for her charming cottage – Mark Homewood for his dynamic apartment and loft – June and Jon Summerill for their precious studio in Paris.

I would also like to thank – Gilles de Chabaneix for his glorious photography and Richard Boutin who assists – Elspeth Thompson for capturing the spirit with her elegant writing – Meryl Lloyd for her constant support and superb design – Anne Furniss and Alison Cathie at Quadrille – Alfred Munkenbeck and Juan Dols for minimalism – The Designers Guild team before, during and after this book was produced – Jo Willer who assists me brilliantly with my work.

Contents

Foreword

The creation of a home, a private special world in which to live, in my view can be like searching for a more vivid existence, whether it be brilliant minimalist architecture, a period town house, loft or studio. Embracing the dynamic tensions of the city is both fascinating and daunting, full of promise and potential. It is the idealist who takes on the challenge.

Changing the interior of our house from its original role as a traditional town house to that of a contemporary living environment, combined with our wish to live in a space that is both minimal and simultaneously inspiring, generous and full of vitality, presented us with just such a challenge: all-encompassing, yet ultimately immensely satisfying. It has been said that one's domestic environment is a reflection of one's character. Initially, one searches for the concept, formulates the vision, then tackles the vital practical issues. The process of confronting and solving problems, meeting deadlines, taking courageous decisions can be soul searching, painful, but fulfilling. That same process is echoed when working with like-minded people, helping to stimulate their dream-making potential.

I hope that these pages capture the vision. They attempt to reflect the valuable, emotionally satisfying process of making individual spaces that are not finished, static objects but which continue to move and grow with our lives.

Tricia Guild.

"Men came together in cities in
order to live. They remain together
in order to enjoy the good life."
Aristotle, *Politics*; 4th century BC

Rejoice in

Say the word "city" and what do you see? A bustling street market, the air thick with traders' cries and

neighborly gossip? The hub of the financial quarter, bristling with tall glass towers and men in dark suits? Or

a sunny Sunday in the park, the city's inhabitants slumped in rows of striped deckchairs, while streams of

children and dogs weave a procession in between?

Perhaps you see a city from history: Rome under the Emperors, the St. Petersburg of the Tsars, or the

pinnacles of some timeless, nameless city of the East, arising from the desert like a mirage. Or maybe you see

it through the eyes of a writer or a painter: Dickens' London, Baudelaire's or Manet's Paris, the wit and angst

of Woody Allen's New York, the luminous anonymity of Hopper's late-night bars. Generations of artists have

found in the city a potent metaphor for the human condition: for its splendor and its squalor, for our

sociability as well as our fundamental loneliness, for fortunes to be made, dreams fulfilled and forgotten.

the city

Cities have always been exciting places to live, full of contrasts and extremes. Ever since the first cities were raised from the Middle-eastern mud, they have acted as magnets for the agents of change and renewal; marketplaces for the exchange of new ideas as well as a trade in goods and services. Cradles of our civilization, they have been seedbeds of revolution in everything from politics and philosophy to art and architecture, fashion and entertainment.

Modernity and change are woven into the fabric of city life. The way most cities grow is organic—sprawling and contracting, different neighborhoods rising and falling—continually adapting themselves to the demands of their inhabitants. Old buildings may be pulled down and new ones put up, but the past is never erased; it is there to be traced in the name of a street, the carving above a doorway, an old pub sign. Ancient and modern co-exist— as do beautiful and ugly, rich and poor, sociability and alienation—often within the space of a single street.

Common criticisms of the city are that it is noisy, polluted, and dangerous, and there is no doubt that this century's emphasis on economic expansion, and in particular the rise of the automobile, have done nothing to enhance its allure. All too often, urban living is regarded as a compromise—convenience and accessibility constantly weighed against the disadvantages of congestion, uniformity, chaos, and grime. Town and country can become polarized in our imaginations until the countryside has a monopoly on space, on solace, on soul. But it doesn't have to be that way.

Problems there may be, but there has seldom been a more exciting time to live in the city. Recent years have seen something of an urban renaissance take root throughout much of the western world, from splendid public art and architecture projects in Paris, Stuttgart, and Seattle to the redomestication of parts of the financial districts of London and New York. Contemporary parks and river walkways are opening up brave new urban vistas everywhere from Barcelona to Newcastle. Measures to fight pollution are being considered, and some cities are already leading the way in curbing car use and creating energy-efficient new transportation systems. Many planners (including the British architect Richard Rogers, who has devised an exciting scheme for the heart of London) are striving to realize a new vision of city living—sustainable in economic, cultural and psychological terms—that can take us into the next century and beyond.

The time has come to celebrate the city and to find new ways of living in it. The key to urban living is to rejoice in urban virtues. Let go of the rural idyll: the need for friends and flexibility, for constant change and challenge, that the city fulfills can be as crucial to well-being as acres of unadulterated green. From elegant town houses and cozy mews cottages, to docklands warehouses and rooftop aeries with chimneyscape views, the city offers an exciting variety of living spaces. More recently, former industrial buildings are being converted into stylish new loft apartments, providing exciting expanses of space at affordable prices, right in the center of town. All of these can easily be adapted to fit a modern way of life.

The city home is an ideal place to develop a new definition of modernity. No retro nostalgia here, no rural hankerings in the form of dried flowers in your kitchen and wall-to-wall chintz. You don't need a modern

"The city does not tell its past, but contains it like the lines of a hand, written in the corners of the streets, the gratings of the windows, the bannisters of the steps, the antennae of the lightning rods, the poles of the flags ...."
Italo Calvino, *Invisible Cities*, 1972

"Cities have changed so much that it is hard to remember they exist first and foremost for people .... We should be reinvesting in the idea of a dense and socially diverse city ... focusing communities around lively neighbourhoods."
Richard Rogers, *The Reith Lectures*, 1995

house to have a modern home; all you need is a modern attitude. When decorating, don't deny the city; rather, distill the best of its essence and bring it inside. Think of the way a city grows: of the organic mixture of old and new, of the exciting melting pot of cultures—and reflect this in the arrangement of space, the choice of materials, the incorporation of contemporary arts and crafts. Let your home resound to the rhythms of the city. While a country house is about long, lazy weekends, home life in town is knitted into the fabric of the city and shares its constant comings and goings. It needs to be accessible and adaptable, able to open up for an impromptu summer lunch party, but also to provide a peaceful haven from the pace and pressures of the world outside.

This new vision of urban living is about much more than mere decorating—it is part of the general shift in attitudes that is affecting us all as we edge toward the end of the century. Just as in fashion, where padded shoulders and power dressing are now a thing of the past, the mood in interior design is also moving toward something softer, more soulful, and much more individual. Making a home is not a matter of what you put on your walls or how you hang your draperies. It is an emotional response to your surroundings and the way you want to live. For Tricia Guild, it is also where she experiments with the colors and textures, forms and ideas that will inspire her next collection of fabrics and furniture.

For twenty-five years, as the founding director and creative force behind Designers Guild, Tricia Guild has been at the cutting edge of contemporary interior design. Her innate ability to mix vibrant color and pattern and her imaginative use of modern arts and crafts translate particularly well to the challenges of urban living. A passionate urbanite who flies frequently between the world's capitals, she rejoices in the rich visual stimulation and dynamic energy of the city. Her country house in the hills of Tuscany is a beautiful refuge for relaxing with her family, but London is her permanent home. It is also the international base for Designers Guild, from the bright and busy shops in the heart of the King's Road, Chelsea, to the converted Victorian printworks north of Holland Park that houses the creative team, sales, finance, and production staff. Tricia Guild's new London house, a short walk from the office and within easy reach of the lively antique

markets, museums, and galleries, smart restaurants and street theatre that animate the city, is the perfect illustration of her vision of urban living.

On the following pages, photographs of Tricia Guild's house show how using the inspiration of the city can create the ultimate urban home. Visits to a variety of other city homes she has decorated or helped to inspire—all owned by like-minded people who share her vision of city life —demonstrate that the ideas can be adapted to very different spaces, from a family town house to a tiny artisan's cottage, a New York apartment to a Parisian pied-à-terre, the perfect one-person hideaway to the skyline sanctuary of a brand-new London loft.

"It's all about old meeting new.
Very few people build a new
house in the city – one chooses a
certain space with a certain
character and the challenge is to
dance off that character, adding
individuality in the process."
Tricia Guild

A space in the city
Tricia Guild's London home

Tricia Guild's London house is the ultimate illustration of her new definition of modernity. It is also perfect proof that you don't need a brand-new building in order to create a totally modern living space. Just as in the ever-changing modern city, old and new co-exist in a series of exciting contrasts—the spire of a medieval church reflected in a skyscraper's plate-glass windows, a piece of modern sculpture animating an old cobbled street—Tricia Guild has taken this strong urban mixture and made it part of the very fabric of her home. Her radical transformation of a large Victorian family house did not begin with a ruthless ripping out of its traditional features; nor, of course, has it involved a thoughtless veneration of the past. Instead, an exciting tension between old and new runs through the house like an electric current.

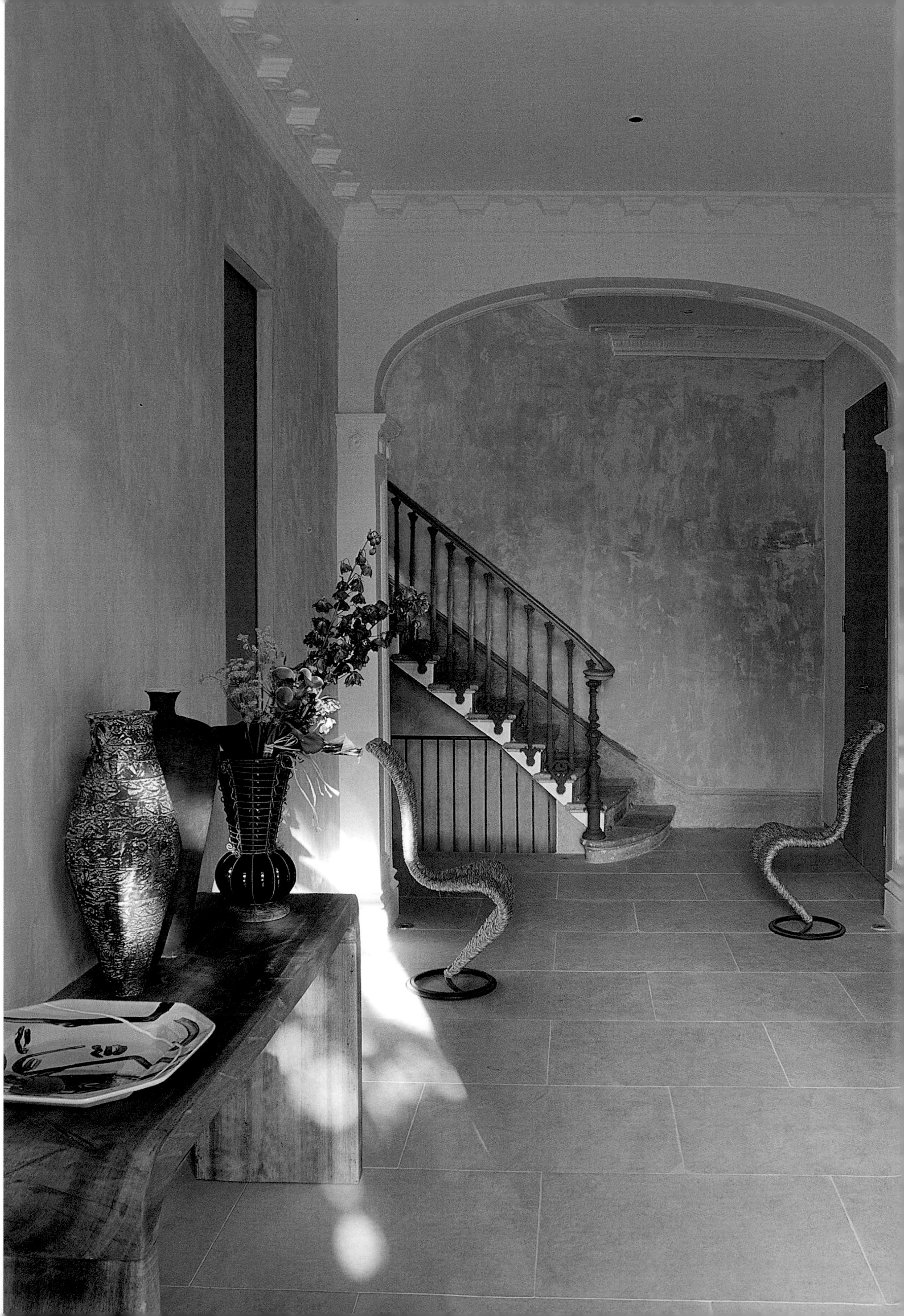

The bright, airy entrance hall sets the scene with its exciting combination of old-meets-new. Walls decorated with the swirling color and texture of a contemporary abstract painting butt up against original cornices, their convoluted moldings painted crisp white, like the icing on a wedding cake. Traditional arched windows are left bare, their plaster surrounds suffused with zingy lime green, to make sunny niches for contemporary arts and crafts; modern ceramics and sculptural flowers create a warm but unusual welcome.

At the very heart of the house, the original freestanding staircase, its ornate iron balusters painted a flaming orange, provides the strongest visual metaphor for the fantastic fusion of old and new that runs throughout the house. At the top, a plain round glass skylight throws ellipses of light around the stairwell, marking the passage of time like an interior sundial.

light

color

texture

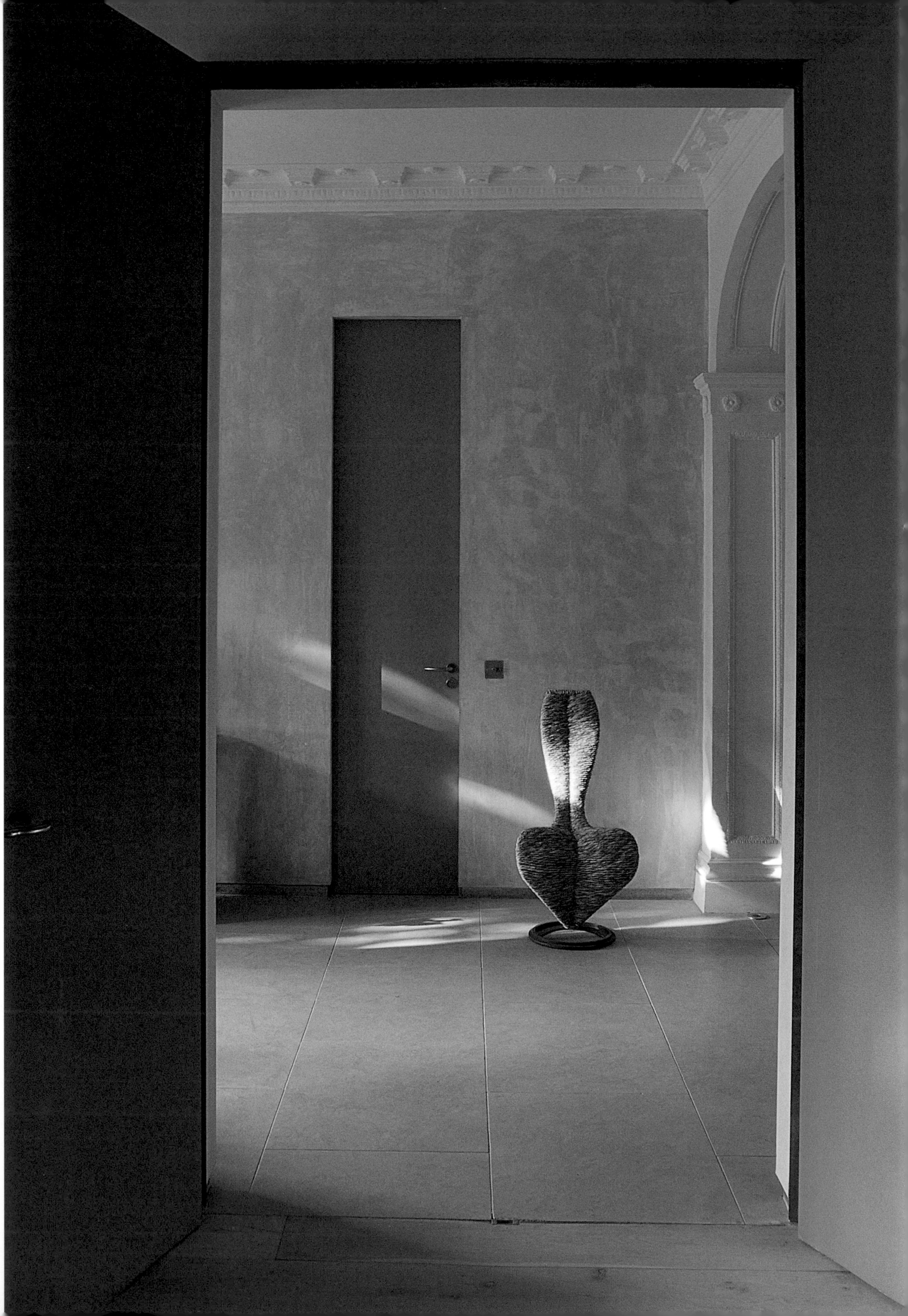

Still in the entrance hall, tall, narrow doorways accentuate the natural elegance of the house's proportions. A raffia chair by Tom Dixon stands sentinel at the entrance to the downstairs bathroom—a tiny space brought alive by cobalt-blue mosaic tiles, contemporary arts and crafts and a single, sloping sheet of glass that makes an intriguing washbasin.

tall doorways, open space

Off the hallway, the airy, glass-roofed studio/sunroom is where
Tricia Guild comes to work and think as the ever-changing light
throws patterns around the bright blue walls. Neither indoors
nor out, the room opens onto small terraces at both the front
and the back of the house, and can be looked down on from
the arched stairwell window.

Like many others in the house, the studio walls are suffused
with swirling color, applied to the raw plaster while it was
still wet. They make a dynamic backdrop for favorite books
and treasures, such as ceramics, embroidered textiles, plants,
and flowers collected for inspiration. In summer, an armchair
and table can be taken outside for a view over the garden.

sunlight through glass

organic

patina

ceramic

crafted

handsewn

indigo

orange

The studio/sunroom is an example of how one can create new and exciting spaces while still remaining sensitive to a building's original architecture. From the front of the house, there are few signs that such a thoroughly modern room exists behind the sunny roof terrace. Slanting slashes of glass in the roof make for maximum light all year round, while preserving the privacy that is so vital to life in the city. Here, one of the glass panels butts up against the arched window in the stairwell, framing a view down onto Tricia Guild's private world.

Space to live in

Old houses were built for a very different way of life. Until recently, large houses, both rural and urban, tended to have different rooms for specific purposes: drawing rooms and dining rooms, parlors and pantries—not to mention nurseries, sculleries, and servants' quarters. For most of us, life in the modern age is much less structured, and some degree of adaptation is usually necessary to make a successful contemporary home. Some of the latest urban architectural developments—from the conversion of an old Parisian train station into the Musée d'Orsay to the transformation of former riverside warehouses into apartments and restaurants along London's Butlers' Wharf—suggest how sensitivity to the past can go hand in hand with stunning modernity. In Tricia Guild's house, respect for the generous solidity of the mid-Victorian architecture has not prevented the opening up of the interior almost to the limits of structural feasibility, while new spaces, such as a book-lined study and the studio/sunroom, have also been created.

When Tricia Guild and her husband came across this house, it had like so many larger town houses been converted into apartments, its graceful proportions clumsily carved up into small compartments. Despite this, she could see the potential to open up the original larger space and create an almost minimalist canvas which she could then color in and bring to life. The result is a stimulating environment that is at once of the city, reflecting its exciting cultural rhythms, but also apart from it; a place that can accommodate large-scale entertaining as well as informal family life; a dynamic backdrop for contemporary arts and crafts and, in the new studio/sunroom she has created, a reflective space in which she could explore the rich sensuousness of her thoughts about color and texture, recharge her creative batteries and make room for new ideas to surface and distill into form.

In consultation with Alfred Munkenbeck, an architect whose views on the simplicity of space and minimalist detailing she shares, the house's interior has now been re-established as four principal living spaces which are much looser in nature than the original occupants would have been used to; an open-plan kitchen-dining room and seating area on the garden floor; an elegant double living room, study and sunroom off the hallway on the raised first floor; the master bedroom, bathroom and dressing rooms occupying the whole of the second floor, and guest bedrooms and bathrooms in the former staff bedrooms up at the top. Changing the position of some of the doorways has produced a flow of movement that now suits a more contemporary way of life. Tall, narrow double doors accentuate the main rooms' dramatic high ceilings; in the bedroom where no elaborate original cornicing remains, these stretch right up to ceiling height. The upper floor bedrooms retain their original intimate charm.

"The house has a strong, organic blend of neutral textures and materials with exciting color— the two are interfused so that rather than being a distraction, or an end in itself, color forms part of the texture and pattern and emotion of the space."
Tricia Guild

Light

On the lower floors of the house, the aim has been not only to open up the interior space itself, but to extend it, both psychologically and visually, out into the gardens at front and back. In earlier times, for safety, comfort, and security, houses were designed to shut the door on nature and the elements; these days, particularly in the city, if you are lucky enough to have a green view, it makes sense to bring it indoors. In the kitchen, the coved brick ceilings of what was originally the cellar, held up by the slenderest of steel verticals, stretch all the way from the front wall to the back, which has been replaced by a bank of six galvanized metal and glass doors. Sun streams down through six skylights, throwing lozenges of light onto the pale stone floor; this same surface is continued out into the terraced garden—another device that extends the room beyond its physical dimensions. With steps up and away from the house, bordered with pots spilling over with flowers, the garden provides its own organic screen from neighbors and passers-by. In the living room upstairs, elegant French windows can be thrown open onto a metalwork balcony overlooking the public gardens beyond, while slashes of glass in the roof of the sunroom/studio open it up to the changing sky. And at the very top of the house, the introduction of a plain round skylight throws welcome shafts of light into the stairwell.

Color and

Cities are often perceived as gray and soulless, but where there is color, it sings out all the more against a neutral backdrop. Think of rows of bright vegetables on stalls in a city square, the flashing of neon against a night sky, the peeling layers of film and theatre bills on an old brick wall. The streets are full of inspiration for using color in the urban home.

Tricia Guild has brought alive the cool, open, almost minimalist framework of her new house with an exciting new fusion of color and texture—rich and organic but completely contemporary. Seldom is color seen as a flat, inanimate surface. The walls vibrate with flat swirls of pure pigment sunk into the raw plaster as it dried, or flash with the glint of thousands of tiny mosaic tiles in cobalt blue, lime, or orange. On the wooden stairs and top landing, the stripping back of layers of paint suggests an abstract, striped finish—at once strikingly modern and totally in keeping with the original attic style. In the top bedrooms, asymmetrical plains and stripes blur into one another with all the quiet beauty of a Rothko canvas.

Certain colors recur like themes in a musical score: the lime green of the hall reappears on the far wall of the living room and again downstairs in the kitchen; warm blues were chosen for the master bedroom and

texture

the sunroom; accents of orange run from the kitchen up to the topmost bedroom, their progress followed by the orange staircase itself. There are striking contrasts as colored walls meet at corners, as a pink room is glimpsed through a lime doorway; as the curlicue arm of a blue chair sings out against a warm pink backdrop. The vibrant mix of color might seem overpowering were it not for the vital part played by the countering neutrals and naturals.

Tricia Guild's use of bright color works because it is balanced. The living room in this house may be turquoise, but not all the walls have been colored. There are planes of white plaster which allow the colors to breathe and, paradoxically, increase their impact. The floors are pale stone or bleached wood, and the paintwork is either white or a soft blue-gray, creating space and light around windows and doors and making a neutral buffer between rooms and the spaces beyond. Other neutral textures incorporate something of the urban aesthetic: acid-treated zinc in the kitchen fixtures and etched glass and brushed chrome in the bathroom have a semi-industrial feel that contrasts well with the painterly use of color.

cobalt
vermilion
indigo
magenta
orange
mandarin

"Most people have a strong personal feeling for color. It's important to trust and be sensitive to one's own intuitive color sense— discovering it is challenging, stimulating, and creates dynamic and positive energy."
Tricia Guild

Looking from the hall to the living room: a modern mix of color and texture brings striking individuality to the large double room, while the original crisp cornices and subtle, sculptural pieces of furniture emphasize its elegant proportions. Tricia Guild's use of bright, vibrant color is balanced by the use of white and neutrals. In the spirit of the Mexican architect Luis Barragan, not all the walls are painted turquoise, and plenty of white around the windows increases the feeling of light. The clean, modern framework has been colored in with contemporary furniture, arts, and crafts. Modern ceramics echo the rich, rubbed-down textures of the stairs and walls, and textiles vary from gold-printed crushed linen to pale natural sackcloth embroidered with string. This is the most formal space in the house, but the unexpected juxtapositions of colors, styles, and materials prevent it from becoming remotely stuffy. The urban living room is often required to adapt to different situations; Tricia Guild's is equally suited to a large cocktail party or a quiet afternoon reading in the calm, diffused light by the window.

relaxed elegance

The modern city home is the ideal place to display contemporary arts and crafts. On the previous pages a graphic metal fireplace and grate by Tom Dixon becomes a showcase for ceramics by Linda Hoffhines, while here, small multicolored pots by Henriette Gaillard are a microcosm of the rich color scheme of the entire room. A snaky copper lamp echoes the curlicue arms of the Marouska Metz chair, while modern paintings sing out against the swirling abstract texture of the walls. The bright, vibrant palette embraces the colors of contemporary art but also of nature. Attention to detail does not mean making things fussy: flowers are simply and wittily arranged; cushions are trimmed with contrasting braid or simply sewn with string. Throughout the house, curtains are banners of natural sackcloth, frayed at the edges and simply embroidered; in this room, they are complemented by a single, asymmetrical drapery in lime green crushed linen printed with gold.

At the other end of the living room, the introduction of orange and red to the color scheme and the inclusion of a pair of curvy, overstuffed armchairs have created a comfortable, slightly less formal feel. Reflecting the rich cultural diversity of the modern city, the stripes of bright color on a contemporary painted cabinet and handwoven rug hold a suggestion of India or Turkey, while at the same time appearing totally of the here and now. This is a place to sit and listen to music or read by the light of the French windows leading to the garden.

lime raspberry sapphire turquoise

The city home often has to act as office, too. Off this end of the living room, a small, raspberry-pink study has been created, lined with shelves full of books. Bright colors and interesting textures, in everything from furniture to textiles and stationery, create a dynamic atmosphere. As warm and intense as those in a Howard Hodgkin painting, these colors have a strong emotional charge which is shot throughout the room, right down to the geometric patterns in the handwoven kilim. A turquoise ceramic-top desk by the window looks out onto the back garden, while small vases of flowers, or sometimes individual blooms, present the opportunity to contemplate nature at close range.

WRITING
1991–93

On the garden floor, former cellars and servants' quarters have been opened up, almost to the limits of structural feasibility, to make an open-plan kitchen, dining room, and small living room leading onto the garden. With its bank of acid-etched zinc cabinets and state-of-the-art cooking equipment, the kitchen has echoes of a smart urban coffee bar or restaurant, but is enlivened by bright fruit and flowers and jaunty plastic utensils and containers.

living

cooking

eating

bright

plastic

zinc

mosaic

café

shiny

At the other end of this floor, a bold contemporary mix of color and pattern brings the dining and sitting areas alive, countered by the natural, neutral textures of driftwood, string-wrapped chairs, and the pale stone floor. The stone continues through the wall of glass doors to the terrace and steps in the garden, an effective device that makes the room feel even bigger and blurs the distinction between indoors and out. For an informal lunch with friends, bright citrus colors, fresh flowers, hand-embroidered napkins, and painted ceramics on a driftwood table echo the palette of the painting behind. Dishes are kept in the big painted armoire, its paneled doors picked out in two shades of turquoise. A bright magenta and orange plaid sofa and shelves crammed with books bring an air of comfort and intimacy to the area of the room focused around the fireplace.

Along the back wall of the house, a bank of sliding glass doors and skylights brings in views of the garden and floods the whole of this floor with light. Centered around a ceramic fireplace by Ralph Levy, the sitting area proves that it is possible to create an intimate area even in a very large space. In summer, the glass doors can be opened onto the pool and fountain outside, while in winter, the focus is inward – the addition of a kilim in earth colors makes the area a place to curl up with a book in front of a log fire.

checks

stripes

skylight

The continuation of the same pale stone floor out through the glass doors assists in the illusion of bringing the outside in and extends the space of the dining room out to the garden. A square pool, with a blue ceramic base and a simply designed fountain, is reminiscent of the clean lines and pure color of a modern painting; kidney-shaped stools, and square pots of clipped box and helxine continue the theme.

Modern nature

Living in the city needn't mean losing contact with nature. The rhythm of the seasons may be less obvious than in the country, but it has its impact on our busy lives just the same. The urban garden or terrace is an opportunity to be free with nature: leave cottage gardens to the country where they belong, and experiment with strong shapes and modern ideas. Urban inspiration is all around us, from smart new city parks in Paris and Barcelona to the quirky individuality of painted pots spilling over from balconies or hung from the walls of a secret courtyard, half-glimpsed from the street. Inside the house, by reflecting seasonal changes in the way we use our home, we can add a richness to city life and re-connect ourselves to nature and the earth. At Tricia Guild's house in summer, long evenings spill out into the garden after work—doors and windows are thrown open, curtains are minimal, and the spaces are open and airy. When winter closes in, fires are lit, dividing doors are closed, and draperies have another layer added for warmth and privacy. Throughout the year, the house is full of flowers—just a single bloom from the garden against a contrasting wall can have as much impact as a painting, and fresh fruit and vegetables from the local market are displayed in bright bowls or on open shelves. Wherever you live, the colors of nature are a feast for the soul.

"I am strongly attracted
to the stimulation of the
city—its architecture
and parks, the business
life and the streetlife,
the theatre and markets,
the extraordinary mixture
of people all gathered
together .... The cityscape
is just as inspiring as
the countryside, but is
much more dynamic
and individual ...."
Tricia Guild

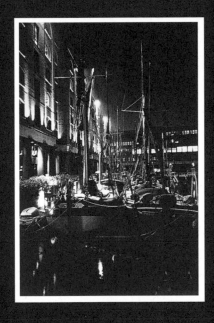

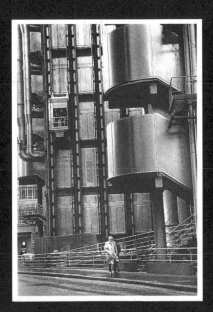

Arts and crafts

Cities are melting pots for cultures from all over the world, and the urban home is the ideal place in which to display contemporary arts and crafts. Loosen the definitions of what is "art" and what is "craft" with glorious glazed ceramics jewel-bright against a contrasting wall, a distinctive fireplace in ceramic or zinc, bright handwoven rugs and other textiles. Hand-crafted objects have real soul appeal: their irregular, organic shapes and textures can raise the energy of a room, even adding something of the romance and ritual of cultures that are quite different from our own.

"In my view, 'modern' doesn't have to mean cold and austere .... I've tried to create a pure, almost minimalist framework and then give it an individual personality using shape, vibrant color, exciting textures, and the organic, quirky qualities of contemporary arts and crafts ...."
Tricia Guild

Tricia Guild has always been passionate about modern arts and crafts. Here, she incorporates them into the very fabric of the house. Contemporary artists Tom Dixon and Ralph Levy were commissioned to design fireplaces for the principal rooms; the graphic metal of Dixon's plays against the more elaborate existing ironwork of the house, while the heavily textured ceramic of Levy's work (he has also made several tables) marries well with the swirling abstract textures of the walls. In the master bathroom, a stone bathtub like some minimalist sarcophagus is glimpsed through sliding doors of etched glass, while at the other end of the room, a bright blue Levy fireplace establishes a more intimate mood. Freestanding furniture is almost sculptural in its appeal—the snaky silhouettes of Tom Dixon's raffia chairs, the curves and curlicues of Marouska Metz's armchairs; even the towel rails look as if they could be bulls' heads by Picasso.

Some pieces seem reminiscent of distant, half-remembered places—the rubbed-down layers of brightly painted cupboards somehow suggest India, the striped rugs Turkey, the low-slung wooden bench and rope bed some nameless Pacific island—while at the same time they appear totally of the here and now. Everywhere there are much-loved paintings and ceramics, carefully placed against a colored wall, to catch the light from a window, or grouped with candles, a handmade book, and fresh flowers.

"The London city, with all its houses, palaces, steam engines, cathedrals, and huge immeasurable traffic and tumult, what is it but a Thought, but millions of Thoughts made into one—a huge, immeasurable Spirit of a Thought, embodied in brick, in iron, smoke, dust, Palaces, Parliaments, Hackney Coaches, Katherine Docks and the rest of it! Not a brick was made but some man had to think of the making of that brick ...."
Thomas Carlyle,
The Hero as Man of Letters, 1840

"An atmosphere can be warm, dynamic, intelligent
and eccentric without being retrospective."
Tricia Guild

Design and detail

It is the details that give a city home soul and make it totally your own. Tricia Guild's approach is to pay great

attention to detail without ever becoming fussy. Materials reflect the character and contrasts of urban life.

Here, baseboards and architraves are of galvanized metal recessed into the wall—a strong modern take on

the traditional alternative but also extremely practical. Textiles vary from utilitarian sackcloth and unbleached

muslin to rich gold-printed silk and embroidery. Pillows and throws make splashes of color on beds and sofas,

their different fabrics, patterns, trims, and embroideries linked in a web of bright color and texture that

becomes a personal signature.

From the second-floor landing, lime green walls give way to the calm but warm blue of the bedroom, where an Indian-looking daybed, strung with natural rope, is heaped with pillows and contemporary textiles all in shades of blue.

blue

natural

string

linen

muslin

silk

cobalt hyacinth indigo azure sapphire sky

The bedroom's serene, all-encompassing blue color scheme is studded with subtle, contrasting accents of pink, lilac, and lime: jewel-bright anemones, handmade beads, handsewn blankets and a tiny, out-of-scale painting by Craigie Aitchison. There is a rich mix of fabrics: the curtains are plain white crushed linen, simply embroidered with string; on the bed, white and denim-blue linen and natural sackcloth are juxtaposed with a contemporary kilim and gold-printed silk throws. Again, the attention to detail is light and simple, rather than fussy and overdone. This sensuous, nurturing space takes up most of the second floor, opening at one end onto walk-in closets to the right of the window and, through sandblasted glass sliding doors, to an airy modern bathroom at the other end. Running across the entire width of the room, the glass doors provide a degree of privacy while also enabling the bathing area to remain warmer than the bedroom.

Their walls painted the same zingy lime as the plastered landing, the pair of walk-in closets prove that organization needn't mean a loss of soul. Floor-to-ceiling rails, open shelves of industrial glass, and sliding drawers keep everything hidden but perfectly to hand; shoes are in neatly labeled brown cardboard boxes, while smaller items are packed in fabric-covered files. Everything is full of the promise of a summer's evening in the city. A lilac silk throw lined with sackcloth and embroidered in string makes for an interesting meeting of textures.

stone

linen

cool

glass

texture

light

calm

The bathroom illustrates Tricia Guild's exciting contemporary mix of dynamic color and natural, neutral textures. Ultra-urban, semi-industrial materials like etched glass and brushed chrome are countered by the organic qualities of stone and wood, then brought alive in a blaze of color down at the far end, where a painted blue wall, a swirling ceramic fireplace, and the rich, irregular shapes of contemporary arts and crafts create a more intimate atmosphere.

at the top of the house

Up on the top landing, paneled doors, board floors, and mansard walls retain their original, attic feel—somehow reminiscent of a young artist's garret in Paris. Bright stripes on the blue floorboards are as vibrant as a contemporary abstract painting; the effect was suggested by the layers of old paint revealed when stripping the stairs and is continued into the bedrooms in the paint effects around the fireplaces and on the simple wooden furniture. In keeping with the architecture on this floor, the furnishings in the smallest guest bedroom are simple: a painted table, an old armoire and a bleached wood chair seem to echo the textures of the walls, while beds and chairs are given stylish but minimal coverings.

mandarin   peacock blue   magenta   citrus green

In the brightest of the spare bedrooms, asymmetrical stripes and planes of color turn the walls into an abstract painting that glows orange in the late afternoon sun. A bold mix of patterns fills the room with energy: soft stripes, large checks, graphic flower prints, and the geometric designs of a handwoven rug. Reds butt up against pinks; orange encounters crimson; acid green with turquoise. The armchair in the foreground sums up the style: its traditional shape has been given a new, jaunty coat in a witty, oversized check, and it suddenly looks very contemporary. A bold tulip print on the bedcover echoes the strong turquoise ceramic fireplace, while accents of acid green make a stunning contrast against the smoldering sunlit walls.

The guest bathrooms are small and compact, simple without being spartan. Two walls are covered with jewel-bright mosaics; the fixtures are plain polished steel. A sculptural towel rail, textured towels, and fresh flowers in contrasting colors strike a more individualistic note.

lime

clean

light

fresh

stone

glass

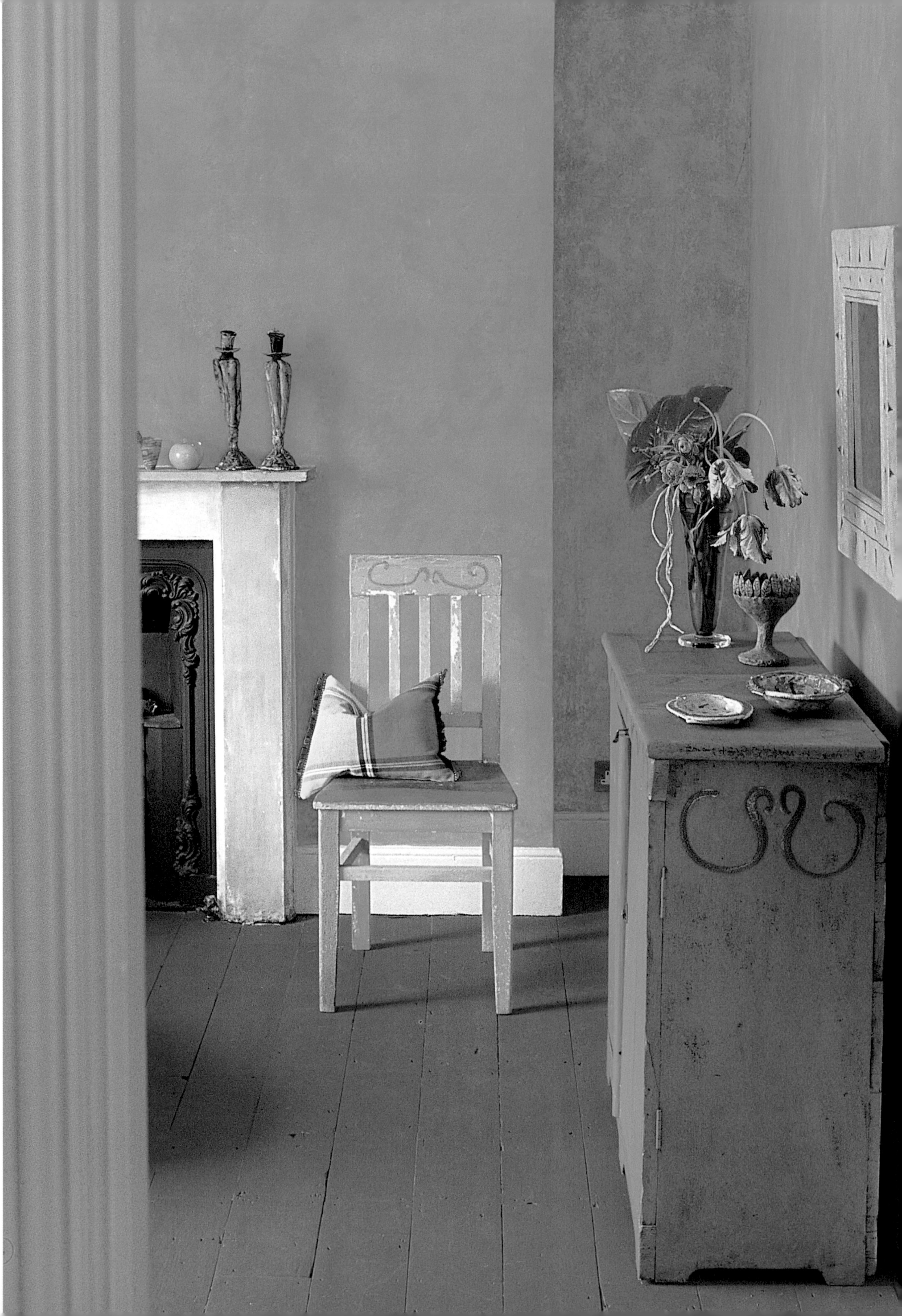

Blue floorboards and simple painted wooden furniture contribute to the breezy charm of this sunny top-floor living room. The aqua-green walls, rubbed and painted in soft hand-drawn stripes, have all the calm serenity of a Rothko canvas—one could gaze at them for hours. Small details prevent the style from slipping over into nostalgia: the crumpled lime linen cover on the chaise longue; the confident handpainted swirls on cabinets and chairs; a crazy leaning spiral metal lamp. Stunning frames and flower vases by contemporary artists and craftspeople sit on the simple fireplace, which is in full blaze every winter. The smallest guest bathroom has cobalt blue tiles—its main form of decoration—and semi-industrial fittings.

"There is great potential
vitality in close-knit urban
communities where social
activity can be spontaneous
and where the necessities
and pleasures of life are
close at hand ...."
Harvey Sherlock,
Cities are Good for Us, 1991

Urban virtues

Tricia Guild's approach to new urban living can provide inspiration for schemes in any of the rich variety of spaces the city offers as home. The houses and apartments, loft and studio featured in the rest of this book all belong to people who share Tricia Guild's vision, and they illustrate the way in which exciting contemporary design can bring something of the spirit of the city into the way we live. The basic principles are adapted to suit each particular case—a clean, new space opened up as far as is feasible for a flexible way of life, the dynamic fusion of color and texture, the rich contemporary mix of old and new, organic and industrial, arts and crafts. Similar ideas, materials, and pieces of furniture crop up again and again, but each scheme is unique—appropriate to place, to a way of life, and above all to personality—a distillation into physical form of an individual's response to the urban environment.

"In the dingiest streets of the metropolis are
to be found homes, the rooms of which are
lofty ... the ceilings beautifully ornamented,
the chimneypieces models for the sculptor ...."
Thomas Beames,
The Rookeries of London, 1850

Living histories

Cities are full of houses that were built for a way of life that no longer exists. Each one tells a story. The
Georgian crescents of Bath, the canalside burghers' houses in Amsterdam, the Beaux-Arts façades of Upper
East Side Manhattan may now form a part of the contemporary urban landscape, but they bring something of
their history with them. Those who are susceptible to these things can sense this contribution in the ghostly
clatter of a horse and carriage pulling off into the night, the call of a street crier above the taxis, the shadowy
figures of girls dressing for a ball in the window of what is now a hotel. Even much humbler homes have a
part to play: the ridges of back-to-back cottages spilling down the hill from the (now disused) factory, the rows
of artisans' cottages where children once played in the street while mothers gossiped in doorways, the cobbled
mews—once stables for the rich houses behind them and later converted into studios by trendy Sixties
photographers. Only modern houses seem devoid of ghosts; but they, too, are products of their age, and their
time will come. Every house is a palimpsest to which we add our own layer of history. The challenge remains:
how to live in such places in a way that suits our contemporary way of life without denying the past?

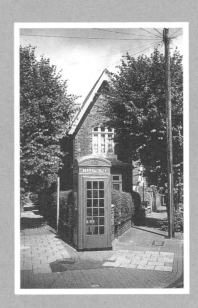

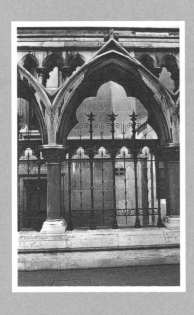

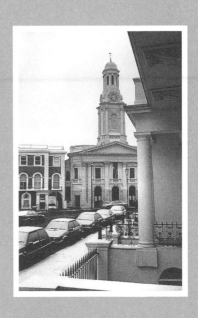

Easy modern living

One of the potential drawbacks of urban houses, particularly those built in the nineteenth century when most cities underwent rapid expansion, is that they can seem so similar: street upon street of Victorian bays or artisans' cottages, all with exactly the same layout inside. Given the chance and the money, modern architects can open up these spaces as never before—changes in lifestyle and methods of heating mean we need no longer rely on a network of small rooms focused around a fire, and advances in building technology offer the means. But even with a minimum of substantial architectural alterations, quite ordinary houses can be revolutionized from within.

A major priority for most modern urban dwellers is an open-plan kitchen and dining area. Separate dining rooms are a relic from a former, more formal era of entertaining; nowadays the kitchen has become the hub of the house, where the modern working cook can prepare the food while chatting with guests over a glass of wine. An old dining room might become a nursery, study, or TV room, while on the lower ground floor, former storage and servants' quarters can be transformed into an airy kitchen-dinette. If the room

opens onto the garden, entertaining can spill outside in summer, with herbs and tomatoes, handy for cooking, grown in pots by the door .

Keep the decorations clean and contemporary; too many English city kitchens try to emulate their country cousins. Raw, unfussy textures and materials rejoice in their urban roots: galvanized metal doors have all the no-nonsense functionalism of a French factory; the sheet-steel gleam of a semi-industrial stove calls to mind the best city restaurants; even the appliances can be streamlined classics from the roll-call of twentieth-century design. An underlying earthiness prevents such spaces from becoming soulless. Pale limestone flooring and raw pink plaster walls form a natural, neutral backdrop against which the vibrant colors and organic forms of vegetables, flowers, and plants fresh from the local market can sing out. Put some poetry into the details: in the crumbly texture of handthrown earthenware pots, or in sackcloth strips, sewn with household string, to hang up at windows or cover dining chairs.

Industrial meets organic

You don't have to buy expensive modern furniture to create a smart, contemporary interior. Just like people, even quite traditional chairs and sofas can be dressed up in jewel-bright linens, exotic swirls, or candy stripes that will sing out in style against a contrasting wall. An adventurous mix of patterned textiles can bring a house alive with all the variety and immediacy of a streetmarket stall: stripes jostle with checks, swirls with curlicues, a geometric rug is placed at the foot of a sofa covered in wide bands of yellow, blue, and green. Again, the secret lies in the use of countering neutrals to provide space in which the connections between the different elements can dance. Working with pattern is like composing a melody: themes must be repeated and picked up elsewhere if the effect is not to be chaos and confusion. Choose flowers whose colors echo the stripes on a sofa; pick out the principal tones in a painting; place plain cushions amid all the pattern to bring in the colors of the hallway or the room beyond.

Slow down the pace in the bedrooms and bathrooms; these are places to start and end the day with a calm clarity of mind. The same color scheme can link the master bedroom, dressing room, and bathroom – pale and restful colors such as powder blue are good for sleeping quarters, but choose tones that are too clear and pure to be insipid pastels. All should be clean and simple, enlivened by contrasting accents of bright yellow, pink, or lime. Windows can be simply treated, with silk plaid curtains tied to metal poles, crushed linen undercurtains or simple roman shades. A sparsely furnished bathroom, pure white with accents of coordinating blue, and a cabinet-lined dressing room, empty but for a slipcovered armchair, provide the perfect calm environment in which to dress up for a night out on the town and wind down afterward.

Contemporary pattern

"The city [consists of] relationships between the measurements of its space and the events of its past: ... the height of that railing and the leap of the adulterer who climbed over it at dawn; the tilt of a guttering and a cat's progress along it as he slips into the same window ...."
Italo Calvino,
Invisible Cities, 1972

The family town house
Strong modern color in a period London home

Injecting some of the color and immediacy of the city into this traditional Victorian family house has saved it from staidness and given it a jaunty, unconventional spirit all its own. Major architectural alterations were confined to the garden floor, where former servants' quarters have been opened up to create an airy open-plan kitchen and dining room where this young family can meet and eat; the rest has been achieved through a dynamic and adventurous approach to color, texture, and pattern. Familiar rooms are made modern with a coat of vibrant, unexpected color; a traditional hallway is decked out in raspberry pink; armchairs and plump furniture are dressed up in exotic swirls and candy stripes. Even quite conventional objects such as mirrors and picture frames are given a quirky, contemporary twist.

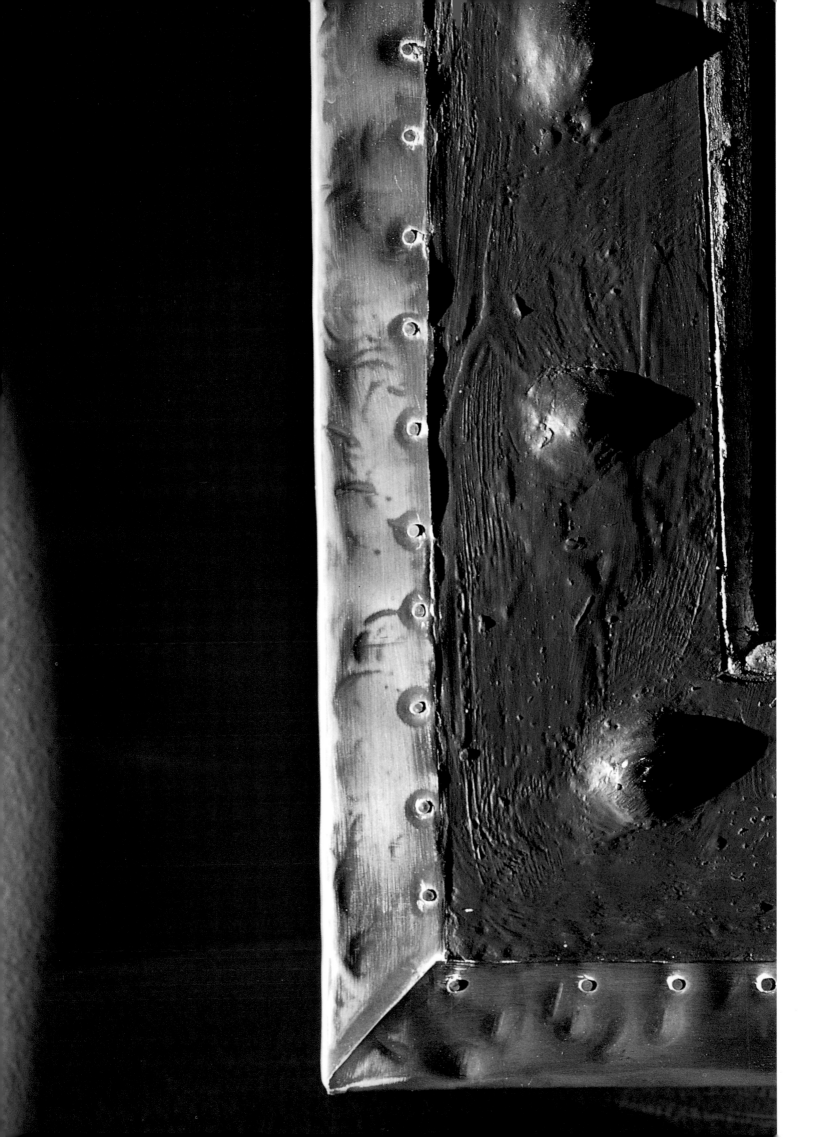

Bright modern color, rather than any major structural reorganization, has given this period family house a bold new look that is totally urban and contemporary. A Schiaparelli-pink hallway sets the scene and provides a contrasting frame for views into the rooms beyond—a lime green study at the rear and the rich cobalt blue living room, with its sherbet yellow and candy-striped furniture. In crisp contrast to all this contemporary color, period details like the original molded cornices, paneled doors, and staircase balustrading are picked out in clean, bright white. With colors this strong, even the balancing neutrals can be more adventurous: coir matting a faded shade of indigo strikes exactly the right note of quiet interest, providing a foil for graphic mats and rugs and forming a modern take on the traditional runner on the stairs.

The adventurous modern mix of pattern in the living room is unified by sticking to a strict color scheme, right down to cushions and ceramics, rugs and flowers. Stripes, swirls, and geometric shapes; lime green, magenta, blue, and bright yellow dance off each other to a rhythm that echoes the pace and richness of the city, from market fruit stalls to modern art galleries.

purple

yellow

cobalt

velvet

canvas

gold

Down on the garden floor, former storage rooms and sculleries have been opened up to create a large airy kitchen/dining room, a small front living room for the nanny and children, and a tiny bathroom. A skylit extension with galvanized metal doors opening onto the garden creates an open, contemporary feel and brings the outdoors inside. This space is endlessly adaptable, moving with seamless ease from a family breakfast to a casual Sunday lunch, to an atmospheric setting for a formal dinner party. There is a modern, urban, semi-industrial feel about the sheet-steel surfaces and gleaming appliances; this is countered by the earthy textures of raw plaster, pale stone, terracotta, raffia, day lilies, and freshly picked fennel.

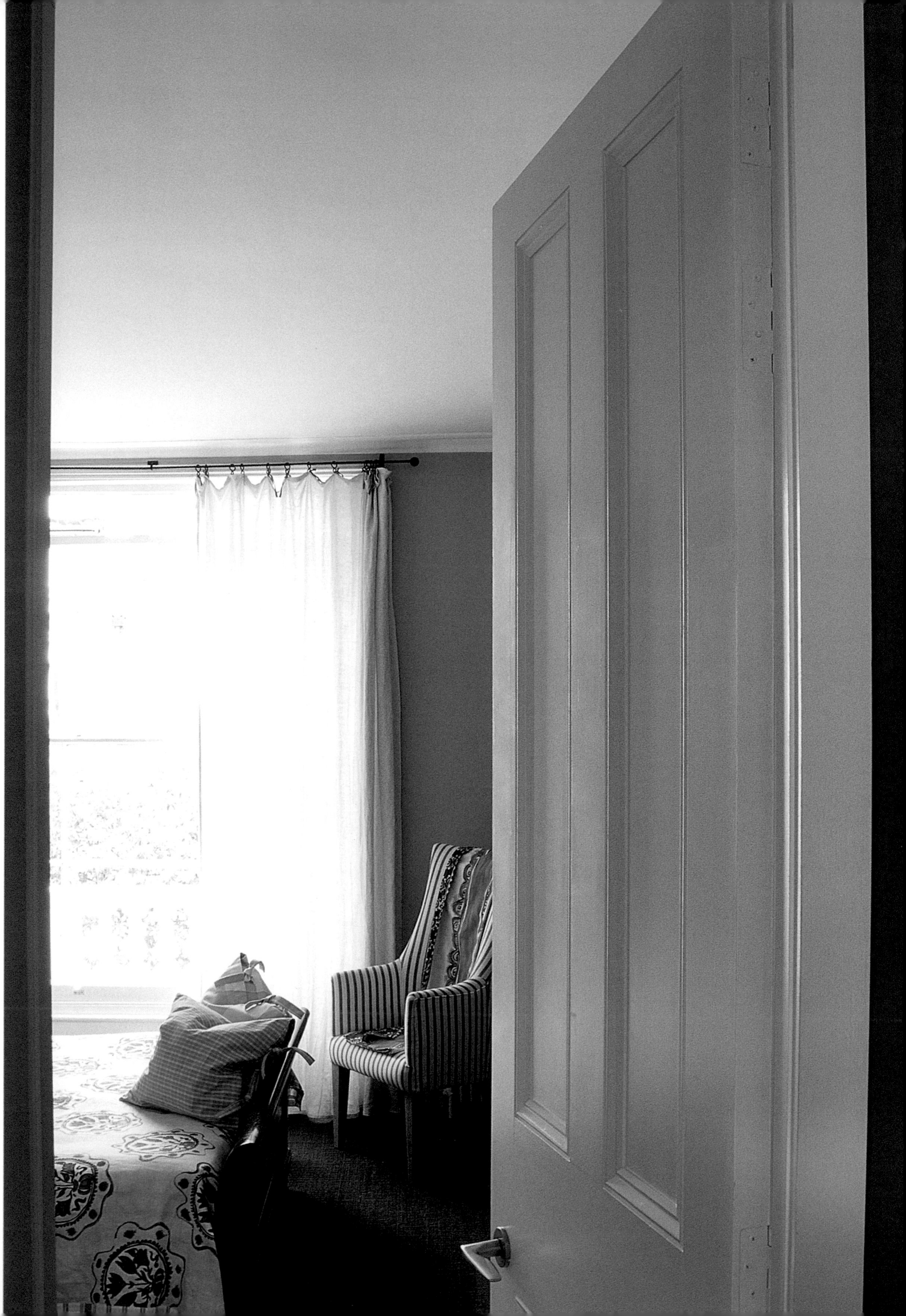

Simple and restful, a powdery blue-and-white color scheme links the master bedroom and bathroom on the second floor. Crushed linen prints and contrasting silk checks at the window make for a modern mix of pattern; bedlinen is crisp white cotton appliquéed with indigo and cobalt. In the absence of built-in closets, wardrobes in blue-and-white painted tongue-and-grooving, with plain thumb-holes for handles, have all the shipshape ease and breezy charm of an English seaside cabin; these are continued into the dressing room beyond.

simple

pure

bright

sky

white

A dressing room lined with wardrobes keeps the bedroom free from clutter. This is the place where a night out on the town begins. The chair, like so many in the house, is a simple classic style dressed up in modern clothes; the pink linen slipcover and other accents of pink refer to the central stairwell, the colorful core that binds the house together.

sky blue

cyclamen

mandarin

lilac

white

indigo

An artisan's cottage
A fresh mix of styles in a tiny mews house

Smaller mews houses and artisans' cottages, which still survive in many of the major cities of the world, make attractive and affordable urban homes for first-time buyers. Built as simple laborers' dwellings or, in the case of mews houses, as stables, they are as close as one gets to a country cottage in the city and, as such, are particularly prone to the lure of all that is rural. How to remain true to the place's urban roots without becoming dull and dreary? How to make such a house modern without denying its humble origins? This tiny terraced house proves that a modern urban home doesn't have to be full of modern urban things; its artistic owners have crammed it with objects that have an old-fashioned, yet contemporary flavor, many of which they have found at street markets or on riverside walks. It is the unexpected uses and juxtapositions that keep the house on its cool, contemporary toes, and prevent it from slipping over into nostalgia. Textures are more important than associations: paintwork is intentionally crackled or rubbed back to reveal the underlying layers; an old table of ancient driftwood is given a runner of crumpled silk; an ornate paste frame, a fragment of molded plaster, and the pitted contours of a favorite fossil form an impromptu tableau on the bedroom mantelpiece.

The living room has been painted bright apple green to catch the early morning sun and form a uniform backdrop for paintings, sculptural fragments, and other treasures. Sticking to a relatively strict palette is advisable in a small space like this: the dusty pink sofa looks good against the green, as does its complementary violet in the silk plaid throw and Roman shades. In keeping with the house's history, the furniture is honest and simple but given an arty, contemporary twist: tables are made from worn driftwood or spindly painted metal; threadbare armchairs have silk throws; cabinets are rubbed and crackled with layers of color.

lime

violet

driftwood

washed

silk

cracked

crumpled

linen

The chalky blue bedroom and creamy white paneled bathroom are saved from countrified nostalgia by the interesting contemporary mix of materials and objects, many of which were picked up in street markets or on the banks of the nearby river. Shelves are made from curly metal or silvered driftwood; a brass bed is draped in a bold modern print; glass bottles, fossils, and fragments of molded plaster are arranged along the top of a fireplace. All the crazy contrasts of the modern city are here, but beautifully and subtly displayed.

Space

The smaller the space, the greater the temptation to go down the retro-nostalgia path: counter this with exciting modern color and an interesting mix of objects. Small urban houses often have no hall, the front door opening straight into the main living room. Confound the expectations raised by the traditional terraced exterior by painting this room a bright, unusual color—yellowish-lime is good if the room catches the early morning sun, or go for cozy deeper tones for a space that is dark all day. There is often a lot of wood paneling in such houses which, if stripped or painted white, can easily smack of the country; similarly, architectural details such as picture rails or cornicing can look fussy and old-fashioned if picked out in contrasting paint, with the effect of making small rooms look even smaller. One solution is to give entire rooms a coat of matte color that embraces all paneling, pipes, doorways, mantelpieces and picture rails; the balancing neutral tones can be provided by the floor—either simple sanded boards or sisal matting. The end result will be an illusion of space and a uniform backdrop against which paintings and other treasures can best be seen.

In keeping with the house's history, furniture should be simple and honest without ever seeming rustic. Spindly metal chairs and tables can be given a coat of unexpected color; a threadbare armchair dressed up with a plaid silk throw. Wood and metal fit well here: wooden floorboards, chunky driftwood tables, and mantelpieces, curly metal wall shelves, cast-iron grates, and bold brass bedsteads and bathroom taps. An imaginative juxtaposition of objects and materials makes the mixture new and interesting.

Reinvention

Inspired by the weird and wonderful contrasts encountered on an everyday walk through the city, one can give traditional objects new uses and bring together products of startlingly diverse origins in new combinations. Like the remains of a building time forgot, fragments of molded plaster become sculptural objects of beauty on the walls. Ornate picture frames are transformed into magical mirrors by the addition of old, foxed glass—kind to the eye and suggestive of ghosts. In the bathroom, a wedge of silvered driftwood from the Thames or the Seine becomes a shelf, a panel of cut crystal from an old pub makes an unusual cabinet. Play with the wit of objects used out of context: old folding garden chairs brought indoors or a turn-of-the-century railroad clock. Everywhere the eye alights there can be food for the senses and fuel for the imagination. As in the world of the real city beyond the door, stories wait to be told, histories lurk under a veneer of modernity. A house can reinvent itself while not ignoring the hold of its past.

"A city is essentially a
meeting of minds, and though
we live in an age where these
minds can telecommute, the
street is still the most visible
face of public interaction."
Peter Jukes,
A Shout in the Street, 1990

"In the Paris of Louis-Philippe,
the bourgeois monarch, the
interior developed its
characteristic role in consumer
society as the realm of private
feeling, private wish fulfilment,
and private display of private
life. Décor might provide what
social revolution had failed
to deliver—the possibility of
each to realise his individual
utopia by populating his
own interior world with the
objects of his dreams ...."
Anthony Vidler,
The Scenes on the Street, 1978

Apartment life

By far the majority of urbanites live in apartments. This is partly due to pressures of space. Over the

last hundred and fifty years of urbanization, four out of five westerners and two-fifths of the world's

six billion population have become city-dwellers; with land in short supply, an obvious solution to

the problem of space has been to build skyward. Some experiments have been more successful than

others. Places with a strong, longstanding urban tradition, such as France and Scotland, have

developed models that are still inspiring today. The Parisian *hôtel particulier,* with its well-

proportioned, high-ceilinged rooms and matronly concierge, remains an ideal model for urban living;

and, for all its checkered history, the nineteenth-century Glaswegian tenement block, with its

communal laundries and play areas arranged around a wide central staircase, is now being revived

as a more sociable and humane alternative to the high-rise block. It is finally being realized that

brutal sky-high boxes, where there is no common space for human interaction save a seedy and

seldom-functioning elevator, are not the answer, providing only a breeding ground for loneliness

and crime.

Much of the history of a city can be gleaned from changes in attitudes toward its buildings and

their different patterns of use. As the social make-up of cities has changed over this century, many

large residences in cities throughout the world have been converted into apartments, the majority of

which are lived in by single people. Former churches, warehouses, and disused office buildings are

now being transformed for domestic use. There is a growing opinion that this is the way forward for

our cities. Rather than expanding endlessly into the suburbs, encroaching on the countryside with

even more low-density sprawl, why not work to re-inhabit the centers? Cities have always

functioned best when their different components—homes and businesses, stores and

angles
lines
curves
geometry
symmetry
grid
circle

entertainment—have coexisted side by side. Medium-density apartments, either above stores, in converted warehouses or in new low-rise blocks, can play an exciting part in the reclamation of the inner city. Living in a well-designed apartment can be the ideal way to enjoy a city. It can provide a personal pocket of space in the center for less cost than a house in the suburbs, a convenient base from which to explore the excitement and facilities on the doorstep and a quiet retreat at the end of the day. For all the joys and stimulation of city living, home is also a haven in which to recuperate, either alone or in the company of one or more close friends. Some city dwellers might set aside a special room, such as a peaceful bedroom on the quiet side of the building, a tranquil bathroom in which to soothe away cares, or a study for reading and undistracted thought. We all need a place to dream, where warm colors and talismanic treasures can transport us to imaginary worlds, leaving us refreshed and rejuvenated and ready to begin life anew.

"Whosoever leads a solitary life,
and yet now and then wants to
attach himself somewhere, ...
according to changes in the time
of day, the weather, the state of
business and the like ... he will not
be able to manage for long
without a window looking out
onto the street ...."
Franz Kafka, *Meditation*, 1913

Home as haven
The perfect urban hideaway

Of the city, but one step removed, the ideal urban apartment is a space from which to observe the life of the streets without getting caught up in it. Perched above London's lively Portobello Road market, these few rooms over a busy shopping street have been transformed into the perfect urban hideaway. Totally anonymous from the outside, its entrance an unmarked doorway on the corner of a row of stores, the interior reveals a self-contained, private world. Rich in color and sensuous beauty, it is a warm red cocoon in which its young owner can forget the rest of life, forget who she is and lose herself in favorite music, books, and paintings. The sunny roof terrace is a voyeur's paradise where one can sit, completely hidden from view, and enjoy a calm perspective on the hustle and bustle below.

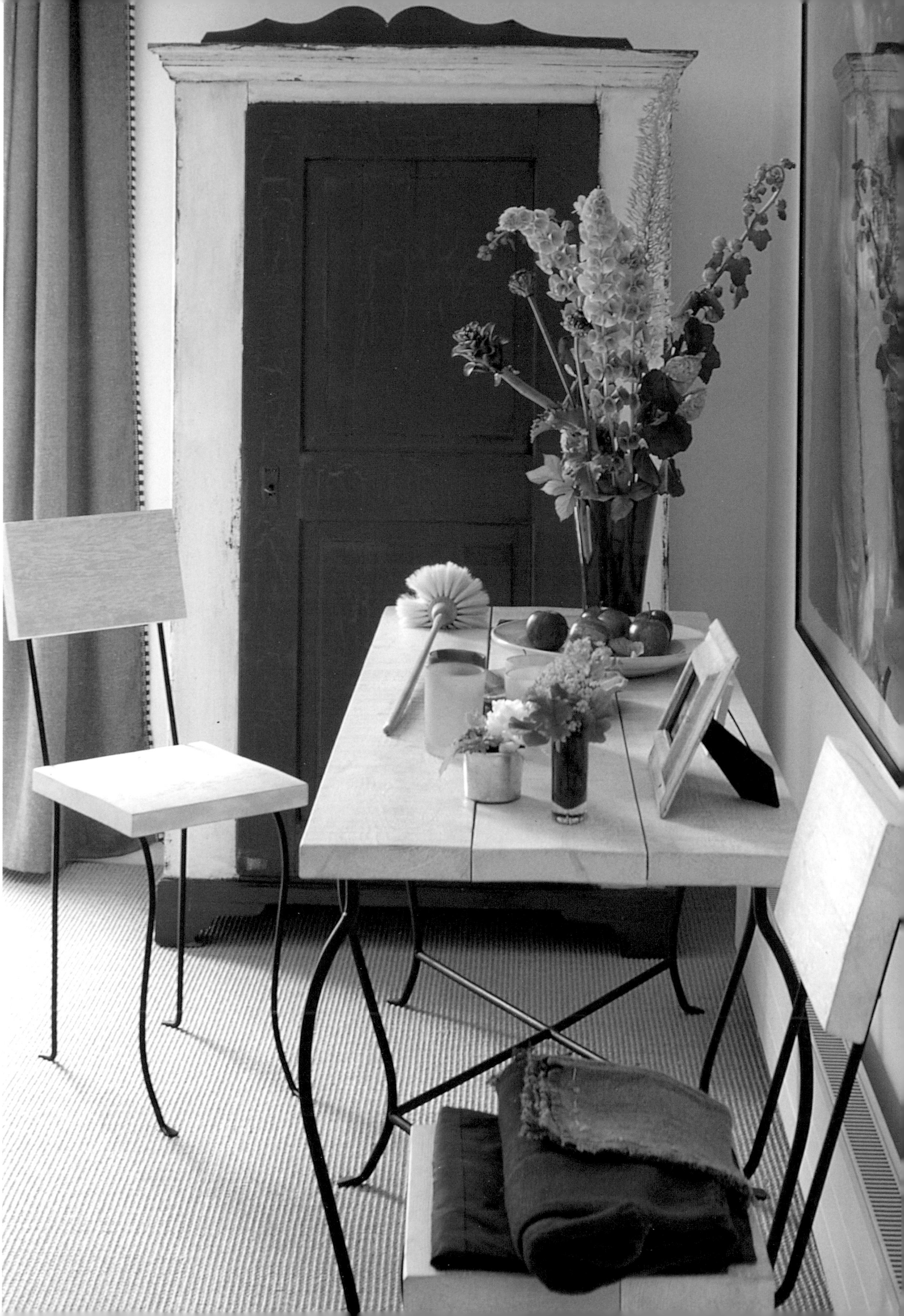

In the living room—by far the largest room in this tiny apartment—white walls and upholstery, natural sisal flooring, sackcloth curtains, and bleached wood have created a calm, neutral canvas which has been enriched and enlivened by accents of deep red and its complementary acid green. Favorite paintings are displayed on the walls or on the wide alcove shelves, which also provide a home for books and handpainted ceramics. One door leads into the diminutive kitchen, while French windows can be either thrown open to embrace the sunny roof garden and its views of the city roofscape beyond or closed against the world.

bleached

wood

apricot

sunlight

thyme

mint

fennel

The vibrant color scheme, countered by white and natural, continues into the bedroom, where deep crimson and orange set a mood that is quietly sensuous, nurturing, and cocoon-like. Accessories keep to the same palette, from the bedlinen, a bold mix of checks, stripes, and hand-appliquéed pattern, to abstract paintings, painted ceramics, and a vase of overblown peonies. Like the kitchen, the tiny bathroom is a feat of design: pale stone, bleached wood, sandblasted glass, and plain white ceramic create a calm and soothing space in which to unwind or prepare for the day ahead.

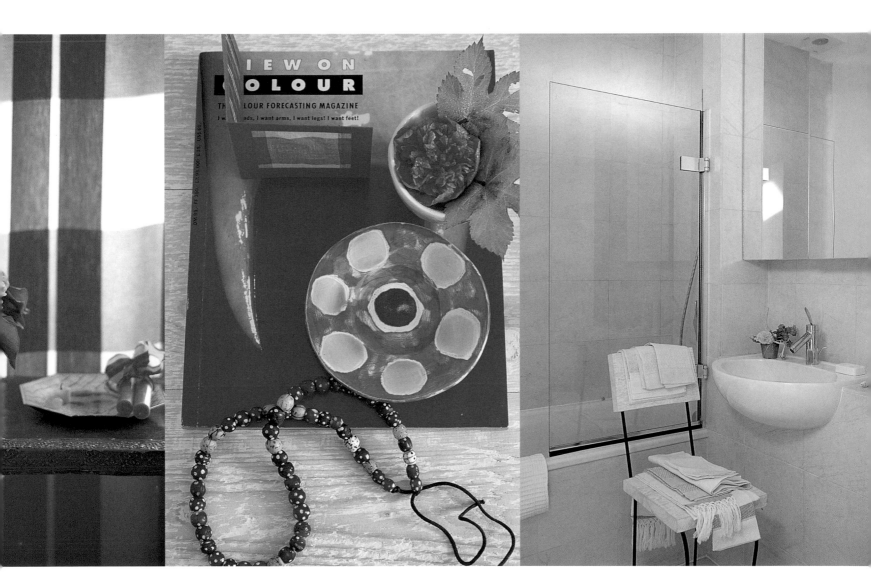

color in a small space

A brownstone apartment
Contemporary arts and crafts in Uptown Manhattan

Apartment buildings are a microcosm of the city itself: a high concentration of different people brought together in one place, all getting on with their own individual lives with varying degrees of contact and cooperation. For all their comfort and convenience, they can sometimes seem soulless places, but even the most anonymous space can be redeemed by bringing in something of the surrounding culture. The essence of a place is distilled into its arts and crafts, and the history of urban America can be traced in the beautiful handmade objects that have brought individuality and style to this collector's apartment in an Uptown Manhattan brownstone. A pair of painted wooden masks seems to embody the heady excitement, urbane wit, and ethnic diversity to be found in a city such as New York; hung at head height on a clear blue wall, they are powerful, provocative, pregnant with stories for the telling. Alongside objects that speak of the country's more immediate past, others tell a tale that is centuries old. Totem-pole imagery brings in the history of the Native Americans, while simple wooden furniture, reminiscent of the rural crafts of the Shakers, is given a witty twist as it adapts to life in the modern city.

EVID 194... RICH... AVEDON

HARO AVEDON EVIDENCE 1944-1994

The terracotta and lime
living/dining room is a
dynamic backdrop for the
fruits of the city:
contemporary arts and crafts
as well as fresh produce from
the market.

terracotta

turquoise

tomato

totem pole

shaker

Planes of
contrasting color,
painted furniture,
and sculptures
made from wood
and newspaper
animate the
entrance hall and
connecting spaces.

"On any person who desires such queer prizes, New York will bestow the gift of loneliness and the gift of privacy ... for the residents of Manhattan are to a large extent strangers who have pulled up stakes somewhere and come to town seeking sanctuary ...."
E.B. White,
Here is New York, 1948

Living it up

New York has always had a strong urban tradition. Perhaps of all the world's cities it is the one that has held, and still holds, the strongest promise of fortunes to be made, dreams to be fulfilled and fun to be had. For this reason it also encapsulates one of the other principal urban traditions: a premium on space. As the modern skyscraper was born, the tiny island rose higher and higher out of the Hudson River in a physical manifestation of its inhabitants' collective hopes to touch the stars.

NY, NY

From high-rise blocks to friendly brownstones, New York offers apartments for every taste. Invented to combine all the comfort and convenience of a hotel with the privacy and permanence of a private residence, the apartment fast became a metaphor for modern city living. To look up at a typical New York high-rise in the evening, the windows lit up in bright rows, is to imagine so many parallel lives, so many personal stories, in many cases united only by the use of the same front door. Many city dwellers love the anonymity of such an existence, relishing their doorstep repartee with the doorman and even the whine of the elevators and—in old buildings—the gurgle of communal plumbing at night. The major down-side in modern blocks is lack of character. The challenge, on taking on such a space, is to make it into a personal, emotionally rewarding home that goes some way toward reflecting both its owner's individual history and its wider cultural setting.

"The island of Manhattan is
a gigantic metaphoric model
of the compression of an
immigrant ship that had
moored and never left. Every
apartment is like a berth.
Every square metre of street
is a deck. The sky-scraping
offices are the bridge ...."
John Berger,
About Looking, 1980

Electric tension

It is unusual to be able to alter drastically the layout of a purpose-built apartment: in most cases the spaces are reasonably well-proportioned and sensibly arranged. Tiny galley kitchens are often a feature; if these can be linked to the main living space by means of a hatch or open countertop this may make for a more sociable arrangement. Even in a one-bedroom apartment, there may be a large foyer with room for a screened-off study area. By far the simplest way to claim such a space as one's own is to make it a colorful modern display case for contemporary arts and crafts.

The higher up the apartment, the better the light, which makes it a good place to experiment with bold and unusual color combinations. Think about using complementary colors, such as rich terracotta orange and turquoise, on adjoining walls, and savor the electric tension where the two planes meet. The other walls can be left white, on which accents of orange and blue can paint their own picture in the form of books and flowers, the stripe of an adjoining tabletop, the graphic brushstrokes of an abstract painting. Lime green for the sofa, a wooden table, and other furnishings complete the three-point base of a balanced color scheme, a rich autumnal palette that makes a dynamic background for a wealth of ornament, both natural and manmade.

"If you would be known, and not know,
vegetate in a village; if you would know,
and not be known, live in a city."
Charles Caleb Colton, *Lacon*, 1820

Soul food

Too many *objets d'art* in a small apartment can make it resemble a gallery shop. The secret is to refine your

collection down to the pieces that have a real reason to be there, both emotionally and aesthetically. Play with

subtle references to your city's history and wider culture—Native American crafts and Shaker furniture in the

United States, for instance; Moroccan or Breton influences in Paris. Bring in your own personal heritage, be it

Irish or African or Eastern European. The modern approach to arts and crafts rejoices in the talents and values

of different cultures, reflecting the social make-up of the city itself. Hand-crafted objects have the most

satisfying impact: a carved swag of fruit and vegetables or charmingly irregular pots and candlesticks bring

their own idiosyncratic energies to bear on a room in a way that no mass-produced machine-made object ever

can. They make the perfect complement for nature's own creations: overblown dahlia blooms, bowls of

bulbous fruit, crinkly-edged cabbage leaves used as plates. Unify the scheme with a coherence of color in

these details, right down to drapery tiebacks, pillow trims, the choice of dishes and glassware, and like a multi-stranded thread it will draw the whole together so that it reads as food for the soul rather than as confusion for the eye.

The same basic principles can be applied to apartments in house conversions. These can vary enormously, from the high-ceilinged *piano nobile* of a grand aristocratic residence to a small row house split into two. A few may be fortunate in retaining elegant proportions and attractive original features; the worst will have been carved up with more of an eye to economy than to quality of space. Again, the answer is to respond to the space that's available: clean it up, make it as compatible as possible with a modern lifestyle, bring in some good strong color and interesting objects. Be bold: if a place is lacking in character, this is the chance to create your own.

Old space, new space

A stylish stage set for urban entertaining

Theatrical color and flair have made the top floor of a once-grand house in central London into a flexible space that can easily adapt to the hardworking, gregarious lifestyle of its stylish male owner. To maximize the light and illusion of space, the main room was painted white and accents of hot color reminiscent of Mexico added in the form of bright ceramics, striped rugs, potted cacti, and painted furniture. Like a stage set, the space can be changed at the drop of a hat to fulfill a variety of functions: study, private living room, or party setting. Clean, uncluttered, and businesslike by day, it can later be transformed, with the aid of an extra folding table, bright dishes, flowers, and candles, into a magical, sociable setting for an impromptu dinner party. In summer, the windows are thrown open to bring in the dappled patterns of the London plane tree outside; in winter, an open fire throws shadows across the walls and the mood is more cozy and intimate. The bedroom is flame orange, a striking contemporary setting for ethnic artefacts and the huge antique sleigh bed that holds the center-stage.

textiles

mexican

leather

cactus

stripes

hot lime   tangerine   blue

The kitchen is refreshingly unstructured: dishes and provisions are kept in a large painted armoire or displayed on the open shelves. One wall has been painted hot lime, a contrasting backdrop for brightly colored paintings and furniture. Galvanized metal cabinet fronts, lamps, and a miniature garbage can bring in some of the raw, semi-industrial feel of the city, while there is a cheerful individuality in the old-fashioned stove and in the handpainted ceramics, bright food packaging, and fresh produce neatly arranged on the tiered blue shelves.

enamel string clay zinc ceramic

Fiery orange establishes a sensuous mood for the bedroom, which is dominated by an antique wooden sleigh bed dressed in Egyptian cotton, raw orange silk, and sackcloth throws. Talismanic objects sing out against the brightly colored walls: Indian miniatures, an old foxed mirror, carved stone figures, and other finds from abroad. Deep blue-green, the near complementary of orange, makes a striking contrast in the form of a painted wooden cabinet, its crackled and rubbed surface somehow suggesting India or Mexico. The dynamic mix of old and new, ethnic and indigenous, luxurious and utilitarian is endlessly enriching. Across the hallway, beyond the tiny bathroom, a small, private study is lined with books and files.

With its black-and-white tiled floor and sturdy, traditional fixtures, this bathroom has a classically masculine atmosphere that is reminiscent of a smart metropolitan hotel. Simple, banner-style curtains in bold crimson and white add some strong color, as do blue glass and bright towels.

Urban nomads

The city's population is always shifting and moving on. Few people, particularly the young, stay in one place for long; the average occupancy of an urban apartment is around two years. For this reason, living in one is often a case of making do with what one has. Few people have the money or time to make extensive changes, and if the apartment is rented, such work may be counter to the lease. This does not mean resigning oneself to a boring, impersonal box: one can claim the place as one's own by means of one's possessions and how they are arranged. Decorating a space like this becomes more like creating a stage set. Neutral or colored walls provide different backdrops against which furniture and freestanding sculpture and plants can perform. The stars of the show are your personal objects: distinctive painted furniture, paintings, ceramics, and plants. Rather than spending time and money on built-in shelves, let large painted armoires hide everything from books and files to hi-fi. In the kitchen, use galvanized metal to cover the doors of existing cabinets and allow hand-crafted ceramics, attractive foodstuffs, and fresh fruit and vegetables to create their own decoration on open shelves. Free-standing furniture can easily be moved. Like actors in a play, who can perform again on a different stage, old furniture will find new roles after a move.

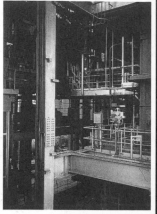

"We should be reinvesting in the idea
of dense and socially diverse cities ...
shaping cities into compact forms and
focusing communities around lively
neighborhoods ...."
Richard Rogers,
The Reith Lectures, 1995

One-room living

One well-proportioned space in an exciting location makes a better foundation for modern urban living than a rabbit warren of small rooms elsewhere. From tiny rooftop studios above elegant city squares to cavernous lofts in an old canalside factory, some of the most interesting urban homes consist of little more than one large room. Whether large or small, it will have to adapt to a variety of different functions: living room, study or office, place for entertaining. The kitchen may be hardly more than a counter top, and unless there is a mezzanine, the space will also have to incorporate a sleeping area. It requires a degree of ingenuity to make such a room cozy and nurturing for oneself and spacious enough to accommodate lunch for twenty.

Well-chosen wall and floor coverings can help define different areas. This might be achieved simply by some mosaic tiles behind the counter-kitchen, a patterned rug beneath the dining table, or a length of embroidered textile on a wall. Furniture may have to fulfill more than one function: a sofa may fold out into a bed, a cluttered desk by day can become a dining table by night. Two matching tables can be united to make a large one and a stash of folding chairs kept in a closet is always useful, as are stools that double up as small tables. Armchairs can be focused around the fireplace on an intimate wintry evening or pushed back against the wall to make space for a birthday party.

Endless adaptability

"It is not given to everyone to bathe in the
multitude: to enjoy the crowd is an art ...."
Charles Baudelaire,
Petits Poèmes en Prose, 1861-2

The city is a great place for impromptu entertaining. In the country, far-flung friends must be invited well in advance, but fellow urbanites can drop by after work, or come in for supper after a night at the theatre or movies. Spontaneity is part of the rhythm of the city.

When so much time is spent in one room, it is important to make the sleeping area a refreshing contrast. If it is a separate space, give it a completely different color scheme and, as a relief from the activity and stimulation of the main area, keep it calm and uncluttered. If it is part of the main space, mark it off with movable screens, or establish another mood with an embroidered bedspread, a handmade candlestick, and a few particular treasures on the bedside table.

Open space

For many people, especially the young and artistic, the loft—a large, open-plan conversion in a former light-industrial building—represents the ultimate urban home. Infinitely more spacious than most conventional apartments, a loft offers a central location, a high degree of flexibility and fashionable, gritty, inner-city charm. Those whose hearts are in the country could never be happy in a loft. The phenomenon began in downtown New York in the 1960s and '70s, when artists and photographers set up homes in near-derelict factories and warehouses. In the past two or three years, as the worldwide recession has rendered more and more inner-city office and industrial buildings available at affordable prices, the practice has spread to Europe and is currently taking London by storm.

Most loft spaces are sold as empty shells of around two thousand square feet, with plumbing for a kitchen and separate bathroom. The best retain some of their former industrial character in the form of steel girders, bare bricks and old metal fire escapes. But what does one do with such a space? How can one define areas of different use without the conventions of doorways and walls?

Once the excitement of open-plan living has palled, more than one latterday loft dweller has reverted to convention and installed so many walls and room dividers that a normal house might well have provided a better alternative. Living in a loft is essentially one-room living on an enormous scale. Making a floor of an old factory feel like home takes practice and a degree of trial and error. Again, the theatrical, stage set approach can be effective. To a certain extent, furniture has to define the space. It should be large and bold enough in style to do the job; small-scale pieces and fussy antiques will look like dolls'-house furniture at sea. Part of the point is to change things around, so fit legs with casters for ease of movement. Wall and floor treatments can also suggest different "rooms". One corner, for example, might have the plaster left raw to define the sleeping space, or the dining area could be given a backdrop of pure, clear color. Thoughtfully positioned rugs can also be used to mark the beginning of new areas. Where extra privacy is required, for example in the sleeping area, make screens to act as planes of pure color; the "rooms" thus formed can be expanded or contracted at will and the movable "walls" provide colorful backdrops for contemporary arts and crafts.

Room at the top

Mastery of space in a smart new London loft

In true urban tradition, the owner of the modern apartment featured on page 168 has now pulled up stakes and moved to a fashionable new loft, bringing many of his familiar possessions with him. With its raftered ceilings, bare brick walls and fire escape stairs, the seventeen-hundred-square-foot space bears witness to its former life as a nineteenth-century varnish factory, but has been transformed into a colorful modern home with character. Different materials have helped delineate areas of specific use: orange mosaic tiles form a backdrop to an industrial sheet-steel kitchen, and glass bricks screen off the tiny, blue-tiled bathroom. The rest of the room can be rearranged according to mood and function: its owner can relax after work with a drink in front of the fire, or sit with friends around the dining table, enjoying the view across the rooftops. Two large sofas and striped rugs have helped define the different spaces, while simple colored screens on wheels divide off the sleeping area and provide interchangeable backdrops for sculptural lamps and plants.

The steel girders, fire escape, and bare brick walls of this large new London loft remind one of its semi-industrial past, but the look has been softened by giving the wooden rafters a wash of white paint and bringing in some hot, vibrant color. Large, bright sofas and boldly striped rugs articulate the main living space, while the kitchen is defined by a wall of mosaic tiles and the sleeping area by the blue "wall on wheels." Nature is not forgotten: mature plants have an almost sculptural appeal, the large cacti echoing the strong verticals of the girders. The double fire escape doors, now painted a zingy acid yellow, can be thrown open for the ultimate urban view of the city skyline.

mosaic

peppers

marigold

hot red

shiny

metal

blue brick

orange

plastic

industrial

turquoise   zingy   tangerine   acid yellow

blue   natural   brick   shiny   steel

Urban ingenuity is tested to the full when creating a sleeping area in a brand new loft, and the antique sleigh bed from the previous apartment (one of the owner's favorite pieces), now presides over a totally new environment. Wooden screens, painted bright colors and mounted on casters, make mobile "walls" that can enclose the sleeping area as loosely or intimately as is required. A different color used on each side of the screen makes for an instant change of décor, and provides contrasting backdrops against which plants and pieces of furniture can be displayed to dramatic effect. Because the loft had no built-in closets, clothes are kept in amply-proportioned armoires painted hot contrasting colors such as lime and turquoise, shocking pink and cobalt blue. The blue-tiled bathroom is screened off from the main space by a wall of glass bricks like oversized ice cubes, which let the light through at the same time as ensuring privacy.

"I know of no other city in the world where it is more agreeable to walk along in a reverie than Paris .... How sweet it is to take advantage of the present moment, then to be lulled by the movement and murmur of a city at once mad and subdued, where the unforeseen has always reigned supreme .... Paris wants to live, it wants to live more than anything."
George Sand

A studio in the eaves

Capturing the spirit of Paris in a rooftop pied-à-terre

In the busy, late twentieth century, many urban dwellers flit from city to city for work as well as pleasure. A small pied-à-terre, even one tiny room, is the ultimate alternative to a hotel, your own personal slice of the city in which to wind down after traveling and tap into your new surroundings. This rooftop studio in Saint Germain in Paris provides all the comfort and familiarity of a home away from home for the professional couple who use it as an occasional base, sometimes together, sometimes alone. A fresh color scheme, contemporary ceramics, and a fine cotton check at the long casement windows let some of the breezy charm of the city blow in and counter the idiosyncrasies of the ancient wooden rafters and shutters. The only interior clues to the precise location are in the tiny details, but the view from the windows could be of no other city.

aqua lemon ecru transparent gauze

As an occasional pied-à-terre, this one-room studio under the eaves has to feel instantly fresh and homely. In the daytime, the windows are thrown open to embrace the city below and let the breezy sunshine breathe life into the delicate turquoise, lime, and yellow color scheme. Breakfast is in the corner café, while lunch from the local caterer can be eaten at a little table looking out across the rooftops. At night, when the shutters are closed and the candles lit, favorite ceramics by Henriette Gaillard and Harriet Thody, books and photographs, plus a vase of fresh flowers from the market in the square below, make this a cozy home away from home.

This view through a casement window is reminiscent of a painting by Henri Matisse. Instantly recognizable, the Paris skyscape is framed by a fine cotton check that lifts and dances in the breeze. What better perch from which to enjoy a private view of this most elegant and artistic city?

**"The City's voice itself is soft
like Solitude's."**
Percy Bysshe Shelley,
Stanzas Written in Dejection,
near Naples, **1818**

Solitude in the city

Old cities, like Paris and London, have interesting, generally accidental nooks and crannies that provide for lives that do not fit conventional patterns. Even the smallest, most unpromising space under the eaves can be made into a pied-à-terre or permanent one-person home. Either through necessity or choice, most city dwellers live alone. French poets in their garrets, and films like Hitchcock's *Rear Window,* portray a rich cultural tradition of solitary urban living. For some people the modern city can seem alienating and overpowering, and the prospect of living alone in its midst daunting and lonely. Others relish the peace and anonymity.

With a small space of one's own, a few friends and a modicum of good spirits, solitary city living can be a source of great joy. Living alone requires taking care of yourself, and your home should help you do this. More than a retreat from the pace of life outside, it should nurture and meet your own practical, emotional, and spiritual needs. Choose your favorite colors and objects, and arrange them to provide intimacy when you are alone while allowing space to accommodate visitors. Take sensuous pleasure in small things: the sunlight slanting in across the floorboards, a dish of peaches, a hand-painted coffee mug. Start the day with breakfast at the local café and end it with supper on the table by the window while evening fades over the rooftops. Shut the door and light the lamp.

Living cities

Cities have always been a focus for visions of the future. From Thomas More's vision of Utopia and the Bible's New Jerusalem to Le Corbusier's Radiant City, and the British New Town movement, the metaphor of the city has been woven into ideal political systems, new forms of architecture, blueprints for new patterns of human behavior. Now, at the end of the twentieth century, our cities are at a turning point. We need to find a new way of living in them if they are to survive in their former splendor and if our all-too-precious countryside is not to be swallowed up by suburban sprawl. We need to fight the tyranny of the automobile, reverse the relentless compartmentalization of residential, retail, and business quarters, save the street market, the city park, and the corner grocery store. More than anything, we need to create new living spaces that rejoice in the diversity of the urban environment and enable everyone to enjoy a modern, enriching, and sustainable way of life. The time has come: cities are for living in again.

"The whole city is a park. The terraces stretch out over lawns and into groves. Low buildings of a horizontal kind lead the eye to the foliage of the trees. Here is the City with its crowds living in peace and pure air, where noise is smothered under the foliage of green trees .... Here, bathed in light, stands the modern city."
Le Corbusier,
The City of Tomorrow, 1929

"Although cities are breeding environmental disaster, there is nothing in the nature of city living that makes this inevitable. On the contrary, I believe that cities can be transformed into the most environmentally balanced form of modern settlement .... In the beginning we built cities to overcome our environment. In the future we must build cities to nurture it."
Richard Rogers,
The Reith Lectures, 1995

DESIGNERS GUILD stockists

Designers Guild fabrics and wallpapers
are distributed throughout the
Americas by the following:

ATLANTA
Ainsworth Noah & Associates Inc
351 Peachtree Hills Avenue
Suite 518
Atlanta, GA 30305
Tel: (404) 231 8787

BOSTON
Shecter-Martin
One Design Center Place
Suite 111
Boston, MA 02210
Tel: (617) 951 2526

CHICAGO
Osborne & Little Inc
Merchandise Mart
Suite 610
Chicago, IL 60654
Tel: (312) 467 0913

DALLAS
Boyd Levinson & Company
1400-C HiLine Drive
Dallas, TX 75207
Tel: (214) 698 0226

DANIA
Design West Inc - DCOTA
1855 Griffin Road
Suite A-474
Dania, FL 33004
Tel: (305) 925 8225

DENVER
Shanahan Collection
Denver Design Center
595 S. Broadway
Suite 100-S
Denver, CO 80209
Tel: (303) 778 7088

HOUSTON
Boyd Levinson & Company
5120 Woodway
Suite 4001
Houston, TX 77056
Tel: (713) 623 2344

LOS ANGELES
Oakmont
Pacific Design Center
Suite B647
8687 Melrose Avenue
Los Angeles, CA 90069
Tel: (310) 659 1423

MINNEAPOLIS
Gene Smiley Showroom
International Market Square
275 Market Street
Suite 321
Minneapolis, MN 55405
Tel: (612) 332 0402

NEW YORK
Osborne & Little Inc
979 Third Avenue
Suite 520
New York, NY 10022
Tel: (212) 751 3333

Designers Guild Bed & Bath
20th Floor
1185 6th Avenue
New York, NY 10036

METRO – NEW YORK
David Parrett
14 East Lane
Madison, NJ 07940
Tel: (201) 635 5545

PHILADELPHIA
JW Showroom Inc
The Marketplace
Suite 304
2400 Market Street
Philadelphia, PA 19103
Tel: (215) 561 2270

PORTLAND
Stephen E Earls Showrooms
2701 N.W. Vaughn
Suite 606
Portland, Oregon 97210
Tel: (503) 227 0541

SAN FRANCISCO
Randolph & Hein
Galleria Design Center
Suite 101
101 Henry Adams Street
San Francisco, CA 94103
Tel: (415) 864 3550

SEATTLE
Stephen E Earls Showrooms
520 South Findlay Street
Seattle, WA 98108
Tel: (206) 767 7220

STAMFORD
Osborne & Little Inc
90 Commerce Road
Stamford, CT 06902
Tel: (203) 359 1500

WASHINGTON DC
Osborne & Little Inc
300 D Street S.W.
Suite 435
Washington, DC 20024
Tel: (202) 554 8800

CANADA
Primavera
160 Pears Avenue
Suite 210
Toronto M5R 1T2 Canada
Tel: (416) 921 3334

BERMUDA
Howe Enterprising
Suite 375
48 Par-La-Ville Road
Hamilton HM 11
Tel: (809) 292 1433

ARGENTINA
Cabello 3919
1425 Buenos Aires
Tel: (054) 802 0850

BRAZIL
Humberto
Escritoria Central
Sao Paulo
R Barata Ribero 263
Tel: (055) 257 3977

CHILE
Rooms Decoraciones Ltd
Alonso de Cordova 3875-3
Santiago
Tel: (056) 207 9150

COLOMBIA
Denise Webb & Associates
Diseño Interior
Calle 79B No 7-85
Bogotá
Tel: (057) 217 1441

MEXICO
Artell SA de CV
Calle 20 No 9
Colonia San Pedro de los Pinos
Mexico 03800 DF
Tel: (052) 272 2861

Fabric, wallpaper, bed & bath and furniture directory

One-off furniture, ceramics and other commissioned work by artists and craftspeople that appear in the book are listed below and are available from the **Designers Guild Store, 267 Kings Road, London SW3 5EN.**

Designers Guild fabrics, wallpapers, bed and bath and furniture (which appear in bold in the following list) are available from the Designers Guild Store and from the stockists listed on pages 204-5. Kalamkari is a collection of wallpapers whose colors and textures correspond to the paint and plaster colors shown on the walls.

TRICIA GUILD'S HOUSE
Hall: Pages 17-23
Wall colors: **Kalamkari** Apple
Whitened plaster: **Kalamkari** Alabaster
Tom Dixon seagrass 'S' chairs
Blue amphora by Ralph Levy
Hand-blown glass and wirework vase

Conservatory: Pages 24-32
Wall color: **Kalamkari** Ultramarine
Paul Anderson reclaimed oak table
handmade for Designers Guild
Ajanta, kilim, handmade seagrass chairs and
low table
Bandhani cotton printed fabric throw on
chair
Ceramics: one-off ceramics by the following
artists commissioned by Tricia Guild: Liz
Hodges, Linda Hoffhines, Edla Griffiths, Ralph
Levy, Henriette Gaillard, Lucy Greenaway
Orange and indigo cushion and throw in
Borghese silk embroidered in string
Philippe Starck Mirto table and Lord Yo
chairs

Living Room: Pages 40-9
Wall color: **Kalamkari** Turquoise
Curtains in natural **Tullow** sackcloth and
lime **Sakumari**, printed gold filigree on
crushed cotton
Curl armchairs in shocking pink **Borghese**
silk
Sofa in white **Killala** weave
Borghese silk cushions in orange and pink
Aripana printed cotton throw lined with
Tullow sackcloth
Lime ceramic table by Ralph Levy to order
Sekordi handmade striped indigo kilim
Linda Hoffhines ceramic jug
Copper Papiro lights

Living Room: Pages 50-3
Wall color: **Kalamkari** Turquoise
Hand-painted antique cupboard
Paint finish by Nick Garrett for Designers
Guild
Duras sofa in orange **Borghese** silk
Balzac armchairs in natural **Killala** weave
Sekordi handmade striped indigo kilim

Study: Pages 54-7
Wall color: **Kalamkari** Rouge
Turquoise ceramic top desk to order
Curl armchair in indigo **Borghese** silk
Patola handmade indigo kilim
Beechwood **Carugo** chair upholstered in
lime **Saffa** chenille
Wool throw by Richard Womersley for
Designers Guild

Kitchen: Pages 58-63
Wall color: **Kalamkari** Alabaster and
Kalamkari Apple
Curtains in pink **Kashipur** woven check
Hand-painted antique armoire

Blue and white Polish cappuccino cups,
selection of olive oils, lime green kettle, table
mats and napkins from Kitchen Department
at Designers Guild

Dining Room: Pages 64-71
One-off handmade oak table and bench
Beechwood basic chair
Sofa in **Tillara** cerise, cushions in turquoise
and orange **Borghese** silk
Throw in **Tullow** sackcloth by Lisa Vaughan
Loge leather chair and stool
Ceramic fireplace to order
Ceramic jugs by Edla Griffiths

Garden: Pages 71-2
Ceramic pond and kidney-shaped stools to
order

Bedroom: Pages 80-7
Wall color: **Kalamkari** Hyacinth
Curtains and bedcover in white **Mahé**
crushed linen embroidered with string Hand-
crafted metal bed
Curl armchairs in lime and white **Mahé**
crushed linen
One-off handmade pink ceramic mirror
Cushions in cornflower and hyacinth
Tandragee muslin

Bathroom: Pages 90-5
Curtains in white **Kilfinny** embroidered with
string
Lime and natural cotton waffle towels and
selection of soaps and bathroom
accessories from Bed and Bath Department
at Designers Guild
One-off lime ceramic fireplace to order
Ceramics by Linda Hoffhines

Small Guest Bedroom: Pages 96-7
Wall color: **Kalamkari** Aqua
Wall painting by Janet and Paul Czainski
Metal Carmelit bed
Schiaparelli pink **Mahé** bedcover in
crushed linen

Guest Room: Page 98
Wall color: **Kalamkari** Tangerine
Wall painting by Janet and Paul Czainski
Hand-painted antique furniture
Pair of antique armchairs covered in pink
Milford cotton check
Zinc bed with banner and bedcover in white
Mahé crushed linen
Throw in turquoise **Mei P'ing** lined with
Tullow sackcloth
Patola handmade kilim
Turquoise fireplace to order

Guest Bathroom: Page 100-1
Curtain in turquoise **Oola** cotton gauze
Waffle towel and bathroom accessories
from Bed and Bath Department at
Designers Guild

Guest Room: Pages 102-3
Wall color: **Stucco** Malachite
Hand-painted antique furniture
One-off handmade ceramic mirror
Candlesticks by Liz Hodges
Throw and cushion in **Kashipur** turquoise
cotton check

Blue Bathroom: Pages 104-5
Curtain in orange **Oola** cotton gauze
Cotton waffle towels from Bed and Bath
Department at Designers Guild

TOWN HOUSE
Hall and Living Room: Pages 112-7
Wall colors: Hall - **Jhati** Cyclamen
Living Room - **Kalamkari** Hyacinth
Indigo and pink runner in hall by Jason
Collingwood for Designers Guild
Curtain in **Jalapuri** checked silk
Trenton chairs in pink and lime **Nantua**
damask
Nashville sofa in red and yellow striped
Lalitha velvet
Curl chair in orange **Kota** cotton canvas
Manhattan sofa in lime **Kusumam** fabric
Patola handmade kilim
One-off candlesticks by Liz Hodges
Metal and slate topped low table from a
selection

Kitchen and Dining Room: Pages 118-22
Wall color: **Kalamkari** Plaster
Cherrywood Banca high stool
Sacramento sofa in natural **Hopsack**
Hand thrown terracotta flower pots from a
selection
Loose covers on dining chairs: natural
Tullow sackcloth, tied with string

Bedroom: Pages 122-5
Wall color: **Kalamkari** Cornflower
Curtains in white **Mahé** crushed linen and
Jalapuri silk check
Bedcover in blue **Ching Pei** printed on linen
Bedlinen: **Millville** and **Winthrop** appliqué
sheet and pillowcases
Atlanta chair in **Tanda** cobalt stripe
Lime **Milford** cushion

Dressing Room: Pages 126-7
Wall color: **Kalamkari** Cornflower
Blind in white **Mahé** crushed linen
Loose cover on **Newport** chair in pink
Mahé
High bleached wood metal Pauvre table

ARTISANS' TERRACE
Living Room - Pages 128-32
Wall color: **Kalamkari** Pale Lime
Blinds: **Jalapuri** mauve and lime check silk
Washed **Jalapuri** silk throw lined in **Tullow**
sackcloth
Cushions on sofa in **Cashel**, **Jalapuri** silk
and **Mahé** crushed linen

Turquoise **Aripana** throw, lined in **Tullow**
sackcloth
Hand-painted antique cupboard
Runner on table in washed emerald
Jalapuri silk
Napkins in lime **Mahé** crushed linen
Ceramics by Tilly Stacey-Young

Bedroom: Pages 134-5
Wall color: **Aviz** Aqua
Curtains in natural **Mahé** crushed linen and
turquoise **Oola** cotton gauze
Bedcover in turquoise **Mei-Ping** printed
on linen
Throw in **Cashel** sackcloth
Lime **Oola** and white **Mahé** curtain on
page 137

HOME AS A HAVEN
Living Room: Pages 144-9
Wall color: **Kalamkari** white
Curtains in white **Mahé** crushed linen and
Tullow sackcloth
Manhattan sofa and floor cushions in
white **Killala** weave
Cushions on sofa in red and natural **Mahé**
crushed linen
Bleached wood and metal Pauvre tables
Hand-painted red and white antique
cupboard
Lord Yo chairs by Philippe Starck and
Adelino table

Bedroom: Pages 150-1
Curtains in pink **Milford** cotton check
Metal Carmelit bed
Banner on bed in pink **Tandragee** muslin
Throw in orange **Ralston** stripe lined with
pink **Litchfield** check
Bedlinen: embroidered red **Milroy** and
appliqué **Redmond**
Pink ceramic top desk to order

NEW YORK
Living Room and Hall: Pages 152-7
Wall color: **Kalamkari** Tangerine and
Turquoise
Curtains in lime **Oola** cotton gauze and
Tullow sackcloth
Sofa in striped **Saffa** lime chenille
Cushions in **Tullow** sackcloth and red
Mahé crushed linen
Chairs in **Lapundra** lime and turquoise
stripe
Throws in washed red **Jalapuri** silk and
Odhni lime printed cotton
Ceramics on table by Linda Hoffhines

Bedroom: Pages 158-9
Wall color: **Pushpa** Almond
Curtains in lime **Mei Ping** printed on
crushed linen and **Tulsk** weave
Bedcover in lime **Mahé** crushed linen
Bedlinen: yellow **Saxton** check and
Millville appliquéd cotton

Index

author's acknowledgements

With much appreciation to the following artists, craftspeople and suppliers: Paul Anderson   Bar Italia   Mick Brady   James Burnett-Stewart   Cappellini   Julian Cloke   John Cullen Lighting   Janet and Paul Czainski   John Derrian   Tom Dixon   John Fennell   Alex Frankl   Henriette Gaillard   Nick Garrett   Lucy Greenaway   Edla Griffiths   Liz Hodges   Linda Hoffhines   Homeier UK   Peter Keegan   Ralph Levy   Loom Company   Terry Lynch   Maroeska Metz   Molesley Refridgeration   Sean Oakes   Orsino   Papers & Paints   A. H. Peck Flooring   Lawrence Pidgeon / Alternative Plans   Pont de la Tour   Pulbrook & Gould   Rainbow Leisure   River Café   Valerie Roy   SCP   SKK   Tilly Stacey-Young   Lucy Stentiford   Sally Storey/Lighting Design   Summerill & Bishop   Linda Thorn   Unidec   Lisa Vaughn   Wandsworth Electrical   Alan Warburton   Wild At Heart   Melanie Williams   Conroy Winter   Richard Womersley

thank you

We would like to thank the following publishers for kind permission to use quotations from their publications:

Aristotle, Politics, translated by T.A. Sinclair, Penguin, 1981

Italo Calvino, Invisible Cities, Secker & Warburg, 1981

Richard Rogers, "The Reith Lectures" from Cities for a Small Planet, Faber & Faber, 1996

Harvey Sherlock, Cities are Good for Us, Palladin Press, 1991

Peter Jukes, A Shout in the Street, Faber & Faber, 1990

Anthony Vidler, The Scenes on the Street, MIT Press, Massachusetts, 1978

Franz Kafka, The Transformation (Metamorphosis) and Other Stories, translated by Malcolm Pasley, Penguin, 1992

John Berger, About Looking, Penguin, 1980

P B Shelley Poems and Prose, Everyman, 1995

Charles Baudelaire, The Poems in Prose, Anvil editions, 1991

Lisa Lovatt-Smith, Paris Interiors, Taschen, 1994

Thomas Carlyle, On Heroes, Hero-Worship and the Heroic in History, University of Nebraska, 1966